THE NORMAL BUT NOT-SO-EASY CHILD

RAISING YOUR CHILD WITHOUT FRUSTRATION, ANGER, OR GUILT

ROBERT J. HUDSON, MD, FAAP

Resiliency Press

All names used in this book are fictitious and any resemblance to real children or families is purely coincidental.

Cover Design: JuLee Brand for Kevin Anderson & Associates

The Normal But Not-so-easy Child/ Robert J. Hudson, MD, FAAP —1st ed.

Library of Congress Control Number: 2019938724

ISBN 9781092482295

CONTENTS

DEDICATION

First, I would like to dedicate this book to my wife, Carolyn, and our children. I consider my wife my greatest teacher and my guide through parenting. My children gave me experience in failure and success. To my parents, for a history of how it was done in my childhood, some good, some not, but with the best intentions and lots of love.

To the parents over the years in my pediatric practice, and to my pediatric partners: you have my gratitude for what I learned from all of you dedicated people.

To all the parents seeking help in understanding their struggles and the struggles of their children, I salute you.

ACKNOWLEDGEMENTS

Writing a book is not a solo endeavor; I am grateful for all the help I have received. To my first outside consultant, Carol Kealiher, for her wise and frank assessment that listening to me and reading my writing were extremely different; she encouraged me to find my writing voice. Thanks to Sean McDevitt, PhD, renowned Temperament expert, for his sage advice and comments. Appreciation to the President of OU Tulsa and author, John Schumann, MD, for his support and encouragement. Many thanks to the editors, designers and publishing gurus at Kevin Anderson and Associates for their encouragement and advice in shepherding this book to fruition. Great thanks are due to Betty Casey, editor of the nationally recognized children's magazine, Tulsa Kids, for reading and offering her experienced editing advice. Lastly, to Carolyn, my partner and wife, English coach, teacher and live-in editor whose insights and intuition are bullseye accurate. Her enduring patience and kindness with criticism are a blessing.

All of you have made this book better.

PREFACE

For over thirty-five years, I have been a pediatrician and helper to parents raising their children. First as a general pediatrician and now as a guide to parents of children who are not easy and who are struggling with behavior and learning issues. During the latter part of my general pediatric years, I was fascinated, humbled, and frustrated as I endeavored to help these parents and their struggling children. There was never enough time to address these complex issues. Parents were overwhelmed, stressed, frustrated, angry and guilty. In my behavioral practice it has been extremely rewarding to see parents after specific consultation help say, "I am beginning to like my child again. He is responding to the tools and plan," or "She seems happier and more competent when stressed." Many of today's parents feel the same way with a pervasive feeling that raising their child is harder than it should be, and they want help and relief. This book was written to share that help from my behavioral practice. First to understand what makes your child tick: his brain wiring. Next to learn new tools, and a specific plan to best manage your Not-so-easy child. You can accomplish this by reading my book. Put the joy back into parenting, Happy reading!

My blog www.drbobsnsec.com serves as a supplement to add current research and topics.

All names used in this book are fictitious and any resemblance to real children or families is purely coincidental.

INTRODUCTION

Why do some kids sail through their childhood while others struggle? Why do some parents seem to have all the answers while others are at a loss to manage their children? Why?

Most parents wonder and worry about their children's future. Most would love to be able to predict how successful they will become. Most parents don't think that prediction is possible, so they are left with only their hopes and beliefs in being a good parent to heal any ill. Current society believes that providing many opportunities for growth is another way to increase the odds of success. Recent research has provided us with rich knowledge to help predict your child's possibilities. These go far beyond hope and make predicting a part of our science and something that you can do with the help of the information in this book.

Can you really predict which children will be easy and which ones will not? If you can predict, how good is that prediction and how early can you accomplish this? Can parents really help their struggling child have success? First, let's explore what we have learned about children. Children are different; "Duh, Papa," as my grandchildren would say. We all know that fact, but still cling to the belief that there is a universal way to parent all children. General parenting advice only works for the easy child. How many of you have an easy child? Most of us need to customize our parenting practices to fit our individual children and their needs. The first section of the book is devoted to helping you accomplish this task.

There are important variables that influence children's inclinations, strengths, weaknesses, abilities, and competencies. Recognizing these skills can lead us to predilections for success or struggles, and exactly how you can help plan what your child needs to maximize her or his success throughout childhood, adolescence, and into adulthood.

Everyone knows the story of people who rise from poverty, a toxic family life, substandard education, and poor opportunities, but, despite all, succeed.

We also have observed children with all the advantages who still struggle. For them, success seems always out of reach. Why?

Some children are more resilient than others. Research shows that resiliency means staying afloat in the face of adversity. Children possess strengths that can promote well-being and protect them against the influence of risk factors. These protective factors create resilience and success in children. If one or all the protective factors are weak, the child struggles.

These protective factors include positive temperament traits and executive functions, superior cognitive ability, and strong families, peer relationships, and fine schools.

Children must draw upon all their resources: temperament traits, cognitive skills, and environmental resources, to successfully counter stress.

The more positive the variables, the more resilient the child. Resilience leads to success; less resilience leads to struggles.

How can you predict if your child will have success or struggles? Please see the chart below.

SUCCESSFUL CHILD Strong cognitive skills, no temperament traits (executive functions) at risk, and a supportive and stable environment **All of these children will succeed**	STRUGGLE-SUFFERING-PRONE ONE variable, either cognitive, temperament, or environment at risk for struggles **These children are struggle-prone**
STRUGGLING CHILD **who may fail if not helped** TWO variables, either cognitive, temperament, or environment at risk for struggles	SEVERELY STRUGGLING CHILD **who is likely to fail if not helped** ALL variables of cognitive, temperament, and environment are at risk

If you are reading this book, you are a good parent who wants the best for your child. I imagine you have strong cognitive skills and a solid loving home, giving your child two of the three main variables in the positive column. However, at-risk temperament and executive functions are major risk factors that determine how a child will struggle.

Here is an example case history of a six-year-old with strong cognitive skills and a positive supporting family, but at-risk temperament traits and executive functions.

Joshua is an attractive six-year-old boy who has shown increasing difficulties at school and at home. His parents are attentive and provide many opportunities for him. He has always been "strong-willed," but he makes good enough grades and his parents excuse his struggles because of that positive. He quietly resists all requests and demands from his parents and teachers. He complains incessantly and has many preferences that must be met or he "blows a gasket." He refuses all things he is not familiar with and has eaten a peanut butter and strawberry jam sandwich for lunch every day for the past two-and-a-half years. He has only one friend, states he doesn't care to socialize with others and prefers to play in quiet pursuits. He is manipulative and stubborn. He seems to have difficulty following through and finishing work. He is curious, full of energy, and loves Legos.

This child is obviously suffering, struggling, and both parents and the child need help.

The information in this book will help parents help children who are struggling, so they can maximize success for that child.

STEP ONE:
PREDICTING SUCCESS OR STRUGGLES

CHAPTER 1

UNDERSTANDING OF BEHAVIOR AND LEARNING

You're Kidding: They Are Not Doing This on Purpose?

Back in the 1950s and 1960s, it was believed that children misbehaved for attention, power, revenge, or from feelings of inadequacy. The same "experts" believed that IQ was the sole determinant of academic success. We now know through neurological research and a better understanding of brain wiring that these early misconceptions are not true.

How children behave and learn is determined by temperament traits, executive functions, and the fit of the environment supporting these children. We now understand the front part of the brain: The frontal lobes are the command-and-control for your child. There are behavior drivers, learning drivers, and integrators that help children navigate this complex world in which we live. How our brain solves problems or struggles to solve problems has been the subject of current research that leads us to know that children rarely behave to get under our skin. Children's behavior is not usually on purpose or intentional, certainly not in the under-ten-year-old; all bets are off for the teenager. There are many brain-driven reasons why some children refuse to obey. Now you're saying to yourself, "Does this mean that my child is not responsible for obeying?" No, absolutely not. A child is responsible just like a child who cannot hear is responsible for understanding what is requested and what is expected, but who can't hear you. Children who struggle to solve problems have a handicap. You would not get angry, frustrated, upset, and yell at a child with hearing loss for ignoring you; you would help that child with his or her struggle by giving the child a hearing aid, and by teaching her to read lips and to sign.

Understanding how your children are wired and what is driving their behavior is the important first step in helping them with their struggles and assuring success, while keeping yourself calm in the process. The child who is struggling in school, but who has a normal IQ, has weak executive functions and skill sets for learning. When we do not understand how our children are wired, we often have unrealistic expectations and are at a loss to help, and cause both the child and parents to struggle. Frustration and anger occur, quickly followed by guilt. This tormenting and distressing parenting occurs when you don't know how to solve the problem of your child's struggles. We say the child is misbehaving, but, in reality, neither child nor parent is equipped to solve the problem at hand. *We now know that the major reason children misbehave is that they become overwhelmed with the demands from themselves, their parents, teachers, sibling, or from a friend.*

A child wants to do what was asked but suffers a conflict in the process of completing and solving that request (problem).

THE BEHAVIORAL CASCADE

The three phases of this failed response to completing and solving the request are as follows. First, lock up; second, meltdown; and third, lash out. The first thing that occurs when children are overwhelmed is that they lock up. During the lock-up phase, their brain is engaged and still working, so they can solve the problem with help. We all know a child's lock-up face: pouting lips, frowning forehead, crossed arms, and generally unhappy demeanor. The less emotional we are as parents, the better we can help the child solve the problem and not fulfill the rest of the cascade. But, often at this phase, the child is pushed to rapidly solve the problem by either himself, his parents, his teacher, or a sibling or friend.

When children are pushed, they move to the next phase of this cascade, which is meltdown. When they are in the meltdown phase, their brain disengages, and they cannot solve the problem. This looks like anything from crying to a full-fledged, foot-stomping, throwing-themselves-on-the-floor fit. When we become angry and upset, we lose IQ points; the experts say as many as fifty points. Most of us would have a hard time solving any problem down fifty IQ points. This is the point where things can really escalate and get ugly. Commonly, the parent attempts to stop the meltdown. However, when you push a locked-up child to "do it now," or to "hurry up," you just pushed him into a meltdown (what I call the mudhole). Picture yourself crawling down into a mudhole. When you try to stop a meltdown, you are figuratively getting into the mudhole with your child. Nothing good or clean comes out of the mudhole. Usually what happens next is lashing out. The child spits, calls you names, claws, kicks, bites, throws things, says he doesn't love you, and generally goes totally berserk. This is most commonly accompanied by a yelling and screaming parent. The parent is also lashing out. Everyone suffers. Overall, a nasty, scary sight. Occasionally, more violence follows, and the child is spanked or punished. Whew, that requires a lot of energy and leaves everybody drained. Guilt follows. All because your child was struggling to solve a problem. All because most parents believe that behavior is intentional. No one would get mad and react this way to a child with hearing loss who throws a fit because she cannot understand spoken instructions. Why do we commonly react in this frustrated, angry way with our own children? Because parents don't understand what is driving the behavior of their child. Remember, a meltdown means the brain is disengaged and cannot solve the problem at hand. The best advice is to "stay away from machinery" and allow the meltdown to run its course without any intervention or discussion. After the child has calmed down, calmly revisit by helping the child to solve the problem.

This may be hard for some parents to understand but will be discussed fully in the next chapter. After you comprehend the behavior drivers and the brain wiring of your child, it will be much easier to facilitate a problem-solving, non-fit-throwing experience. The resilient child rarely has a meltdown and infrequently locks up. The less resilient the child, the more often he or she locks up, experiences a meltdown, and lashes out. Once parents can revise the myth that the child's behavior is intentional, their frustration and anger is replaced with empathy, and guilt vanishes.

We know that there are learning drivers, as well as behavioral ones. When children do not remember what you told them to do the day before, they are not intentionally ignoring you, but rather are having trouble hearing information and getting it stored in their memory for recall later. It is much harder in the learning process to hear information and store it than it is to see information and store it. That is why most schools have smart boards and there is much more visual learning than ever before. If you have a child who is a visual learner and his teacher gives directions verbally, the child will struggle in that classroom. The child is not being lazy, he is not cognitively challenged, but rather he is struggling with some of his executive functions.

The more we understand and identify children's temperament traits and executive functions, the better equipped we are to help a child who struggles with his behavior and learning.

CHAPTER 2

RESILIENCE

Does Your Child Light Up Your House or Blow a Fuse?

Resilience is a word that we hear often these days. What exactly does this word mean, and how does it apply to your child?

In the 1990s, experts defined resilience as the ability to thrive, mature, and increase competence in the face of adverse circumstances. These circumstances may include temperament traits, executive functions, cognitive ability, or the often-blamed environmental neglect or abuse. These adverse circumstances may be chronic and consistent or severe and infrequent. The more resilient a person is, the more the child draws on his or her resources: neurological, biological, psychological, and environmental.

Resilience is the result of your total resources, but it can be improved with appropriate interventions. Some of these interventions occur naturally with consistent parenting. An example would be parents playing impulse-control games at home, such as Mother, May I?

The more resilient a person is, the more successful he or she is. Success changes over time, so competence for an infant or toddler is very different from success as an adult. What we are concerned about in this book is the improvement over time of the neurological, biological, psychological, and environmental strengths present or absent in a child's life as he grows. Each phase of our development requires different strengths. As a child matures, new challenges require the child to use all of her or his strengths. This exposes some of the child's weaker skill sets. We know that working memory, one of the most important executive functions, may not appear as a weak skill until middle school.

Understanding resilience is not always simple because it varies with the challenge. The needs for academic success require a different set of skills than social problem solving. As children face these different problem-solving challenges, all their skills will be needed to be successful. All skills can be enhanced with the proper help from parents. I will be discussing what makes up the skill sets in the form of temperament traits, executive functions, and the impact of the environment on the child.

How does your child react to adversity? Does she bounce back quickly, or does it take a while? Does he stay calm or does he become locked up, go into meltdown-mode, and lash out because he lacks the skills necessary to overcome the challenge? I will explore this complex issue of why your child bounces back in some circumstances and not in others.

Resilience can be measured, and we can predict how each child will react in adverse circumstances. Resilience does not only come into play for large stressors such as the birth of a sibling or parents getting divorced, but for the things that happen frequently every day. How does your child react to a toy being taken away by another child, or not going to the park as promised, or during conflicts with other children, with teachers, with parents, or with siblings? Measuring your child's resilience is the first step in identifying whether you have an easy or a not-so-easy child. *Easy is resilient; not-so-easy is less resilient.*

What are the variables of resilience? As we discussed, there are three main areas. Most parents think that if they love their children and provide support at home, their children will survive anything. This obviously has an impact and is significant, but no more important, and some say less so, than the genetic factor. Within the genetic factors, we all appreciate the importance of a child's cognitive ability. If your child has good cognitive ability and is fairly smart, then she certainly will have less trouble than if she has less cognitive ability. However, we all know children with high IQs who wind up struggling. Why does that happen? The last twenty-five years of research have led us to realize that other genetic factors help determine how resilience plays a role from the start. These genetic factors include temperament traits and executive functions and are important determinants of future success. Your temperament traits and executive functions can be strong or not-so-strong. Identification of your child's temperament traits and executive functioning skills is the first step in determining his resilience. As you learned in the introduction, you must only have one of the three major variables in the at-risk category to struggle in some way.

The past ten years have given us much more information about how your child's brain is wired, and what drives behavior and learning. Many children are resilient in some areas but not so resilient in others; some are whizzes in the academic world but struggle in the social world, or vice versa. A person's frontal lobes are command-and-control for all integrated thinking, both related to behavior and learning. Major variables of this brain action are your child's temperament traits and executive functions. Let's explore your child's frontal lobes to see exactly why this happens.

CHAPTER 3

WHAT FLAVOR CHILD DO YOU HAVE?

Children come in all flavors. Some are a single flavor, several scoops of vanilla, chocolate, or strawberry. Some children are a combo swirl with exotic flavors and a few augmented with fruits and nuts. Some kids are just plain vanilla, plain chocolate, or strawberry. I call these kids easy. These children encompass about thirty percent of all children. A child who is a single flavor is not boring, but these tend to be the children who do as they are asked without much trouble. They are predictable and dependable; they grow and progress without major issues. At the other end of the spectrum are the kids who are not-so-easy, also about thirty percent. These children range from not-so-easy to very, very, very not-so-easy. These are the kids who have flavors that range from mango pistachio to rocky road to cherry walnut coconut. Some are several different scoops at once and some have various toppings. Some are obviously an acquired taste. It's your job as a parent to identify their flavor, acquire an appreciation for their uniqueness, and resist the urge to turn them into vanilla children. The middle thirty percent are easy, with occasional strolls into the not-so-easy behavior. Many people believe that boys are more difficult than girls, but statistically only slightly.

Your child's unique flavor can be determined, and a best-management plan put in place to assure her or him the maximum success by understanding his or her skill sets. You've noticed that I call these children "not-so-easy" and not "difficult," because difficult implies that their behavior is intentional. As I have said before, and contrary to most parents' belief, children do not intentionally do things to get under your skin, create havoc, or "act out" on purpose. We will discuss this concept later, but as you read this book, you will better understand the concept that behavior is not intentional. Children under ten rarely behave to "drive you crazy." Teenagers change to another class altogether and intentionality becomes less of a rule.

So how can you tell if your child is easy or not-so-easy? In less than a minute, you will know. Deciding if your child is easy or not-so-easy is more difficult if it is your first child.

With your first child, you already have an idea of what you want your child to be and accepting the reality of what your child really is sometimes becomes difficult. (But you can always blame the genetics on your spouse...ha!)

Determine if you have a not-so-easy child by following these directions. The score for your child is measured by the number of challenges she/he gives you in a given time period.

This numerical scale is given to each child by the parent(s) using the scale below. A challenge is defined as anything that causes you frustration at home with your child. This can be a refusal to obey, a tantrum, a crying fit, or a meltdown when she/he is frustrated. If your child gives you a challenge two times every month, she/he would fit in the second box, Occasionally Challenging, and you would circle the number below, 3 or 4. If your child causes you to be frustrated every day, then you would circle 9 or 10.

<table>
<tr><th colspan="10">THE NOT SO EASY SCALE™</th></tr>
<tr><td colspan="2">VERY EASY</td><td colspan="2">EASY</td><td colspan="2">Not-so-easy</td><td colspan="2">VERY Not-so-easy</td><td colspan="2">VERY VERY Not-so-easy</td></tr>
<tr><td colspan="2">Never Challenging</td><td colspan="2">Occasionally Challenging</td><td colspan="2">Regularly Challenging</td><td colspan="2">Frequently Challenging</td><td colspan="2">Always Challenging</td></tr>
<tr><td colspan="2">0-1/month</td><td colspan="2">1-3/month</td><td colspan="2">Weekly</td><td colspan="2">1-3/week</td><td colspan="2">Daily</td></tr>
<tr><td colspan="10">Select the number below that matches this child's rating of challenges over time.</td></tr>
<tr><td>1</td><td>2</td><td>3</td><td>4</td><td>5</td><td>6</td><td>7</td><td>8</td><td>9</td><td>10</td></tr>
</table>

Now you know that you have a NSEC and with a 5 or a 9 score you could use some help. There are many other labels associated with these children: strong-willed, defiant, difficult, behaviorally challenged, high maintenance, demanding, high spirited, head strong, troubled, temperamental and spoiled. I believe that "Not-so-easy child" is a kinder phrase to use to refer to these interesting kids. What makes them NSE? We will discuss this in detail using the new neuroscience that helps explain how your children are wired and what makes them tick and causes their alarms to go off.

There are many myths and excuses used to prevent parents from accepting their children as not-so-easy. All of us use euphemisms such as: strong-willed, challenging, high maintenance, spoiled, headstrong or troubled. A common excuse is, *"He's a boy or she's just immature for her age, or he's going through a phase."* This is comforting at the time, but delays parents from early identification of problems and the opportunity to help their children at a young age. I see children often who are six or eight, and sometimes even teenagers, who demonstrated not-so-easy traits as infants. Some children have always been not-so-easy but it's now to a point that cannot be denied.

Neuroscience research during the past ten to fifteen years has given us an understanding of these children and the means to help with their struggles and suffering. We can now help the shy child, the supersensitive or non-sensitive child, the angry, non-persistent, distractible, negative, impulsive, forgetful, defiant, resistant, hyperactive, fit-throwing, struggling, and always-complaining child. We also realize that the easy child needs help. The easy child, who is quite willing to adapt and go with the flow, finds that in doing so, she does not learn to solve problems. This corresponds to the non-adaptive child who struggles with solving problems. All children can be fortified with stronger problem-solving skill sets.

Here is an example of a child who is struggling, but whose parent often thinks that the child is just acting spoiled:

Madison, a cute, brown-haired six-year-old comes down to breakfast planning on having Cocoa Puffs. She has been planning this breakfast since she awoke. She arrives in the kitchen, opens the cereal cabinet, takes the Cocoa Puffs box from the other four cereals available, and discovers that the box is empty. Next, she begins to whine, stomp her feet, and complain bitterly that there are no Cocoa Puffs. She resists all efforts from mom to persuade her to try the other cereals. She may insist that mom go to the grocery now to buy Cocoa Puffs. She is totally stuck and locked up, with only the one answer she has firmly in her mind: "I am having Cocoa Puffs for breakfast." She is suffering; she cannot solve the problem that there are no Cocoa Puffs. I call this "getting to now what." There are no Cocoa Puffs, so now what? It is very easy to conclude that this child is just spoiled. She is not. She is suffering from a problem-solving deficit. This is a common scenario for a child unfortunately labeled resistant and defiant or very spoiled who must have her way. But it is simply the inability to solve the problem of another choice for breakfast. She is stuck with the answer she formed before she got out of bed. This certainly looks like a child who is spoiled and who only wants what she wants. The frontal-lobe reason is that she cannot solve the problem that there are no Cocoa Puffs now, so what do I want for breakfast?

This is an example of a less resilient child who is often viewed as being spoiled or intentionally throwing a fit to get her way, but who simply cannot solve a choice problem. Wow, this is a much different and healthier way to understand how a child behaves. Just this simple understanding of what makes your child tick relieves you of anger and frustration and replaces it with empathy. Not-so-easy children are struggling and deserve our empathy and willingness to help them learn a better skill of problem-solving. The common occurrence is to yell and rant and accuse our children of being spoiled tyrants and ruining the morning for the entire family. How much easier that morning would start if we understood their exact struggle and had several means to help your child solve the problem rather than reacting in a way that gives everyone a churning stomach to start the day. How much happier everyone would be, and the bonus is that your child would learn a better problem-solving skill than the same repeating pattern morning after morning.

Therefore, the first step of predicting which children will struggle is to appreciate the fact that they are not being spoiled or defiant but are locked up and need help. The next step is to identify why.

CHAPTER 4

WHAT MAKES YOUR CHILD TICK?

Why Children Are Different: Your Child's Temperament Traits and Executive Functions

One cold February morning in 1981, I began my pediatric practice day with a six-month-old child who came for a checkup. Entering the quiet exam room, both parents were beaming at their cooing child. Everything was wonderful; he was "so good," sleeping through the night, and on a regular schedule. Both parents were patting themselves on the back for their fine parenting skills. I entered the next appointment room, also for a six-month checkup, and found the baby girl screaming on the treatment table and her mother in the corner, with her tears and mascara running down her face, lamenting that she was a failure as a parent because her daughter seemed to cry all the time. Why are the parents of some infants so relaxed and at ease while other parents are exhausted, guilty, and frustrated with raising their child? Is it because of their parenting skills or is it due to something else? Why do some children:

- Move constantly, while others are content to sit quietly and play?
- Sleep and eat in regular patterns, while others never settle into any routine of hunger or rest?
- Thrive in new situations, while others are shy, cautious, or fearful?
- Focus on one task with determination, while other children jump from one to another?
- Obey quickly, while others immediately resist your requests?
- Laugh and cry with gusto, while others just smile or whimper?

These are some examples of temperament trait differences. Temperament is a natural part of a child's personality and disposition. It is the genetic imprint one inherits. In the late 1950s, two child psychiatrists, Drs. Stella Chess and Alexander Thomas, identified and mapped the following nine traits in infants and then tracked a large group of infants for thirty years. The New York Longitudinal Study is the longest study of its kind to enlighten us that we are not born a blank slate, but rather with inherited characteristics of our parents. You could say it's still your fault how your children turn out, parents, but not because of what you do as much as who you are. Children do start life with a predetermined set of skills. That sounds sort of scary, but it's really a blessing that we can measure and understand what makes your child tick this early. Then there are things that we can do to intervene that will make everyone's life better.

This chapter will explore all the aspects of temperament and how they affect your child's behavior. This focus will bring understanding of why thirty percent of children are very easy and why over half of children are at times a challenge. This understanding is the first step in predicting if your child will struggle or not.

Everyone has the same temperament traits and executive functions. Obviously, people are different, so what makes everyone different? I will be describing the traits individually, but that is not how we experience them in one another. We view others as composites of their traits. Let's use an analogy to help understand how our traits define who we are and how we behave and learn.

For the sake of explanation, let's view ourselves as a combination pizza. We all have the same ingredients: crust, sauce, seasonings, toppings, and cheese. Are you a thin crust, hand-tossed, or deep dish? Does your crust have a lot of flavor, or is it bland? How about your sauce? Too much or too little oregano or garlic, or just the right amount? Are your component ingredients balanced or do some stand out? Is the total bite as it should be or does something stand out and make it noticeably different? So, each of the components alone tastes good, but together it's just a little different. There are lots of different cheeses that can adorn a pizza, but do they combine with the toppings or clash with them? This is how our temperament and executive functions combine to determine a "self."

A pizza contains the same types of ingredients (a person, temperaments, executive functions) but if one stands out too much, the ingredient or trait can be termed "at risk." The degree to which that ingredient stands out determines the amplitude or amount it stands out. A little too much garlic is not the same as an excessive amount of garlic. Human temperament traits and executive functions can also be composed of these excesses. You can say we are like a giant combo pizza.

One of the foremost behavioral outcomes that parents recognize early is how easily the child obeys. Children that are "Not-So-Easy" (NSE) create anger, frustration, and guilt in parents because they become easily overcome and lock up because of at-risk temperament traits. When you have a blueprint of your child's behavioral wiring and a management plan, the family functions in a much happier and more productive way. One dad of four adolescents, two of whom were NSE, came to the office after three sessions and exclaimed, "I've got the key!" He understood how his teens were wired and anticipated their reactions; therefore he was not forced to always react to his children's behavior.

Drs. Chess and Thomas's research proved that temperament changes little over time, but that with help from parents, it can be managed, and skill sets (temperament traits or executive functions) can be modified and struggles turned into skills. By six months of age, these behavioral-style temperament traits are established and functioning and can be measured. At eighteen months, the traits are stable.

Parenting is like driving cross-country. The ease of the trip depends on the automobile, the road, the conditions along the way, and the skill of the drivers. An easy trip would be taken in a large sedan with power brakes, steering, an automatic transmission, and cruise control. If you drove the interstates, read the signs, avoided the eighteen-wheelers and occasional crazy drivers, and lucked out on the weather and road construction, you would not need much driving skill or even a roadmap. If you didn't fall asleep, you would arrive safely, not too fatigued, and without much stress. Forty percent of parents have a parenting experience like that. Their children are temperamentally easy; their "car" (the child) is the sedan with power equipment, and the trip is close to uneventful if they don't run into highway construction, severe storms, or a breakdown.

Sixty percent of parents have a car or child with at-risk temperament traits. These parents will be driving along in a car that they adore, but theirs has a less powerful engine, a stick shift, a tricky clutch, and four-wheel drive. They will make their trip on two-lane roads, with detours, small-town traffic congestion, speed traps, and the same chance of road construction and unpredictable weather. These parents need many more driving skills and a detailed roadmap. Without these tools, parents or drivers are likely to have accidents, become lost, and have unpleasant adventures. The family will arrive at the destination, but all may not have had the trip they hoped for and are worn out from the journey.

Some children's natural temperament combinations are easy, some a challenge at times, and some just plain difficult most of the time. Fifty percent of children are in the category that I call "not-so-easy but normal." Regardless of children's temperaments, parents should love each one unconditionally and should separate behavior from who they are. Parents should appreciate children's differences and consider them in managing their behavior. Understanding this critical information can prepare you, your child, and your child's caregivers and teachers for the likely patterns of behavior that will occur and possibly become a challenge.

The specific difficulties your children may encounter can be predicted according to these combinations of temperament traits. Caregivers and teachers will benefit from knowing children's temperament traits and the corresponding predictable ways they will respond to expectations. This knowledge can prevent situations at home and at school.

Each of the nine specific temperament traits range in each child from easy to challenging. *There is no abnormal temperament, just a range of normal.* Each of the temperament traits was rated low, high, or average on questionnaires completed by thousands of parents about their children. Average ratings mean that the child exhibits a little of both high and low responses. When a child's temperament is rated either high or low, it does not mean that she or he is abnormal but is at risk for behavioral or learning issues and problems that can cause struggling and suffering.

TEMPERAMENT / BEHAVIORAL TRAITS

(From the *New York Longitudinal Study* by Drs. Stella Chess and Alexander Thomas)

Behavioral Drivers

ADAPTABILITY
Flexibility / Inflexibility

- Response to change, transition, surprises, and altered situations
- How long to "get with the program"
- Frustration follows low adaptability
- Thirty percent SLOW to adapt
- Labeled Resistive and defiant or spoiled
- Inflexibility is most difficult temperament trait to manage
- Adaptable: Prone to "go along" with everything and can be too easily persuaded

Hints to manage Low Adaptability: Warn of changes to come; give the plan for the day and the sequence; realize they like to do the same things (play with the same toys). Hang an imaginary sign around these children's necks that says, No Surprises!

APPROACH / WITHDRAWAL

- First response to anything NEW (people, places, foods)
- Curious vs Cautious
- Twenty-two percent LOW or Cautious (Shy, careful, deliberate, wary, resistant to anything new)
- Curious (Bold, risk-taker)
- Cautious is protective but also at risk for social integration
- Curious can be at risk
- Curious: Watch the risk-taker

Hints to manage Withdrawing/Cautious: Introduce anything new gradually and don't push. After the new thing is not new anymore, the child judges for its benefit and not because it's new.

SENSITIVITY (Sensory Threshold)

- Amount of sensory input needed to respond
- Noise, bright lights, temperature change, odors, pain, taste, feel of clothes
- Thirty-five percent LOW
- More prone to colic and sleep disturbances
- More sensitive to low levels of pain
- Feels others' discomfort and empathy
- Twenty-percent HIGH: These children like it loud and spicy and generally are less socially engaged. They may have personal-space issues, poor eye contact, and have a high pain threshold.

Hints to manage Low Threshold: Avoid excessive stimulation: understand their shoes really don't "feel right" and need to be retied. If they are too hot, cold, there is too much noise, or their clothes don't feel right, *it has to be fixed or they will lock up.* These children have more information to process and it takes time and energy. They can be your empathetic children who share feelings with others.

High Threshold: These children have real difficulty with nonverbal communication, social understanding, personal space, empathy, and have a high pain threshold.

Hints to manage High Threshold: Explanations of the *why* of social conventions, play manners, and how to "read" friends' meanings are more necessary with these kids. Explanations may be necessary about why others like or don't like certain things. Stopping a cartoon you are watching together and asking what the character is *feeling* is a good way to realize what this child understands about feelings. Teaching moments may arise from this exercise.

REGULARITY (This is more important under age five and less so over five)

- Body-clock regularity. Some children, you can set your watch by; others, you can't set the calendar by
- How predictable in patterns of:
- Hunger
- Sleep
- Bowel habits
- Twenty-five percent are IRREGULAR: These children are not hungry, sleepy in a predictable fashion, and are impossible to schedule and difficult to toilet train.

Hints to Manage Irregularity: Separate mealtime vs. eating; don't be rigid about eating—these kids may not be hungry at mealtime and hungry in-between on some days. They may go to sleep at six one night and the next at eleven. Naps also vary. Provide quiet-time for those not sleepy. You cannot force a child who is not hungry or not sleepy to eat or sleep. Be flexible.

Hints to Manage Regularity: The super-regular child will lock up if she is required to put off a nap, snack, or mealtime for thirty minutes. Have a plan.

Behavior/Learning Modifiers

INTENSITY

- Energy level of response
- Loud or soft voice
- The "ignore" factor
- Thirty-five percent HIGH
- High intensity = a joy and a pain
- Low intensity = may have needs unmet

Hints to Manage High Intensity: Realize their responses may be exaggerated; avoid responding with the same intensity; do not give in to make peace

Hints to Manage Low Intensity: Take complaints seriously and try not to ignore.

MOOD: This is the glass half-full/positive or half-empty/negative kid.

- Basic mood positive or negative
- Pleasant and joyful
- Unfriendly and a grouch
- Serious, analytical
- Has nothing to do with their happiness, but is their approach to everything
- Thirty-percent NEGATIVE
- Half-empty type fusses, whines, complains a lot, and tends to say, "Oh, that won't work" even before it is tried.

Hints to manage Negative Mood: Don't feel guilty or angry: It's not your fault. Watch for real distress. Learn to ignore and realize every team needs someone to naysay or the untoward will be missed. These children make great auditors.

Hints to manage Positive Mood: Why would you want to manage a positive mood? The super-positive cheerleader tends to ignore possibilities of a negative outcome, which can be dangerous to the child in some situations. The thought that everyone is kind and helpful is a great feeling, but without some reality testing this can be perilous.

Easy-Child temperament traits —Forty percent: The parent-frustration index is low.

- Regular Body Clock

- Positive Approach
- Adaptability
- Mild/Moderate Intensity
- Predominately Positive Mood

Very-Not-So-Easy-Child temperament traits—
Fifteen percent: The parent frustration index is very high.

- Non-adaptability
- Withdrawal
- Low or High Sensory Threshold
- Irregular Body Clock
- Intense/Loud
- Negative Mood

LEARNING DRIVERS

ACTIVITY

- Activity level high or low
- On the Go or Sit and Play
- Restless/confined or content to stay still
- Thirty-percent HIGH
- High **at risk** for disruptive behavior
- Low **at risk** for obesity

Hints to manage High Activity: Provide plenty of exercise opportunities. Send the fidgety one on an errand. Go to the park before the mall or a movie. Always exercise before inactive pursuits. Use physical consequences such as running laps or sit-ups instead of time out.

Hints to manage Low Activity: Make some activity mandatory and limit the high caloric foods.

IMPULSE OR INHIBITORY CONTROL

Inhibitory/impulse control is the ability to resist impulses and the ability to stop one's own behavior at the appropriate time. These are common problems at home and school.

Acts wilder or sillier than others in groups (birthday parties, recess)
Interrupts others often
Gets out of seat at the wrong times
Gets out of control more than developmental age group
Blurts things out
Has trouble putting the brakes on his/her actions
Gets in trouble if not supervised by an adult

Hints to manage Impulse Control: Impulse control expectations start with the child asking permission to talk. "Mom, is this a good time to talk?" Impose consequences for interrupting telephone conversations or conversations between others. Play impulse control games like Red Light/Green Light or Mother, May I. Insist on raising hands for attention or waiting turns. An interruption is lack of brain impulse control. It is not simply about manners.

PERSISTENCE is the ability of your child to stay on task, doing not just what he wants to do, but more importantly a task he doesn't want to do. This trait marks a successful person, identifying those who can do something they do not want to do. Therefore, chores are important; they teach persistence in the face of unwillingness. Persistence is also:

- Time focused on one thing
- Attention span aka impulse control
- Stay with it or give up easily
- Thirty-five percent LOW
- Learning affected by low persistence
- High is focused to finish (Stubborn)

Hints to manage High Persistence: Warn about the need to end activity; reassure that it is okay to leave some things unfinished, and that time will be available to finish later.

Hints to manage Low Persistence: Help organize tasks into shorter segments; praise completion, not speed. Within this category of attention is WORKING MEMORY, an important executive function. Working memory manifests as:

- Staying focused (processing information while listening)
- Staying on task (inhibiting irrelevant thoughts and distractions)
- Sorting information (identifying what is important)
- Remembering multiple steps and those you have already done
- Resisting the impulse to talk
- Storing appropriate information in long-term memory and remembering where it can be retrieved later
- Time management
- Planning and goal setting
- Self-monitoring

DISTRACTIBILITY is the ability to ignore the distractions of noise, movement, or confusion and stay on task.

- How easy is it to divert attention?

- Not the opposite of persistence
- Is it easy to soothe or calm?
- Thirty-five percent HIGH
- Learning affected by High
- "Forgetful" equals high distractible

Hints to manage High Distractibility: These forgetful children need for you to redirect and break things down into an easy-to-remember sequence; first, then second, etc. Most of these kids are visual learners and have difficulty managing multiple-step verbal instructions. Ask them to make a pretend video of the steps and pretend to carry out the multiple steps. This increases the "remember rate."

EXECUTIVE FUNCTIONS

The newer understanding and research of how the brain works involves the concept of executive functions. Temperament is best understood as traits and executive functions (EF's) as skills or processes. Both are present early in a child's life but EFs grow and develop as a child completes childhood. The maximal growth period of EFs is from age three to seven years. Executive is another word for higher order of brain functioning. These EFs are skills which enable the brain to process information efficiently and solve all the problems of living. Each day a child faces social, academic and integrative problems in class, on the playground, after school and at home. They must interact with peers, sibs, parents, teachers and other care givers. Each requires new and changing information containing expectations that aren't always clear to them, but they must navigate these challenges. All these tasks require EFs. The Center for Early Development at Harvard https://developingchild.harvard.edu/science/key-concepts/executive-function/ has a very good video to explain the concept of EFs. EF's function as a sophisticated air traffic control system directing the information arriving in the brain into the proper place.

Like temperament traits EFs have both behavioral drivers and learning drivers. The behavioral EFs are called hot EFs and the learning ones are denoted as cool EFs.

The other executive function is **impulse control** (IC) and is a bridge and necessary component for the hot and cool EFs to successfully operate. IC begins all the thinking processes and helps us to ignore the continuous barrage of information constantly arriving in the brain from our senses. Only a fraction of this information is necessary to solve a problem, so how do we sort it out? IC maintains focus and suppresses what is not useful to solve the problem at hand.

Hot EFs help kids to solve the behavioral issues and involves flexibility or changing course with new information or circumstances. This is called **Cognitive or Mental Flexibility**. Here is an example:

Your child Beth is playing on the playground at school and two friends, Kim and Jane, arrive wanting to play. Kim and Jane are not friends, but each wants Beth to play with them separately. Beth is super empathetic and doesn't want to hurt either's feelings. How does Beth solve this social dilemma?

Temperament traits are the underlying necessary components of hot EFs. The child who is easy, adaptable, and approaching has a better chance of navigating this sensitive situation than the NSE child who is neither adaptable (flexible) nor willing to embrace the new situation.

If Beth had a high sensory threshold and missed the social signals from Kim and Jane, her answer would not be socially successful and further friendships could be jeopardized.

Cool EFs encompass the learning issues and start with impulse control as well. Children with academic difficulty fall into this area.

The first cool EF is to **initiate** the project/process. Unfortunately, society has moralized this skill for the children who have difficulty and label them procrastinators. Initiating a task is an EF, not a moral strength.

The second is **working memory** (WM) and the center of learning. WM is the brain's computer equivalent of RAM. WM processes involve:

- Staying focused and on task (processing information while listening, inhibiting irrelevant thoughts and distractions)
- Sorting information (what is important)
- Remembering multiple required steps and what has been done
- Storing appropriate information in long term memory and remembering where it can be retrieved for later use

The third cool EF encompasses **planning, time management, and goal setting.** All are important skills for successful academic achievement. The fourth is **organization of materials**, represented in orderly back packs, closets and rooms. Those children with weak skills in this area are the "can never find anything" children.

The last cool EF is **self-monitoring**. This skill assures nothing was missed as the child goes back over homework, replays the social problem for better solutions, etc.

Good impulse control and hot and cool EFs are necessary to be successful in navigating our ever changing and challenging world. When children have difficulty with these EFs it is now called Executive Dysfunction. The good news is that with training and practice these skills can be strengthened and the child's struggles lessened.

The Concept of Fit is described by Chess and Thomas. How well your children fit into the world of your expectations and the demands of other caregivers and teachers is determined by these innate temperaments/EFs. Each parent, caregiver, sibling, or friend also has temperament traits, which may be easy or not-so-easy. If conflicts and struggles occur between individual's temperament traits there is a poor fit. A non-adaptive parent and a non-adaptive child lead to daily conflicts and a poor fit. If there is a good fit of temperament trait and parental expectation, then there is harmony, but if there is a poor fit, behavioral problems commonly result. Expecting a very active child to remain still for long periods of time is a temperament-limiting task and a poor fit.

Improving poor fits or tailoring your expectations to the child's temperament becomes the parents' responsibility.

This is the management plan, which is really geared to help the child strengthen weak skill sets. An example is what I call Transition Time. It is a problem-solving process that the parent teaches the child. (See Appendix Help Sheets for details.)

The child is always responsible for his or her behavior. "My temperament made me do it" is not acceptable. Parents who ignore their children's temperament and impose expectations contrary to a temperament trait are really creating the mismatch or poor fit and the resulting problem. If your child displays challenging or at-risk temperament traits, this book will help you to develop a plan. An example of improving the "fit" of a very active six-year-old child whom you expect to sit still for an hour in church would be to run him in the parking lot before entering the church, and if he is squirming midway through the service, to take him into the hall and do jumping jacks for a few minutes. This spending of energy will allow him to remain acceptably quiet until the sermon's end. You have just improved the "Fit." He will respond to that, and the preacher and parishioners will be grateful. Improving the fit is not spoiling the child; it is avoiding a meltdown by understanding his high-energy temperament trait and preventing a conflict between his wiring and your expectation. You are also showing the child that when inactivity is planned, plan activity beforehand.

Recently, during an office session with some parents of a very active five-year-old, her mom asked how to stop her from hanging upside down while eating. I inquired what the child did prior to dinner, and the mom said it's her craft time. I asked how long this lasted, and she replied that it lasted about an hour and a half. I suggested that the craft time be moved to after dinner, shortened to one half-hour, and replace the pre-dinner hour with outdoor activity. You guessed it; this improved "fit" solved the upside-down eating.

Knowledge of temperament is essential to understanding why parenting styles may be required to be different from one child to another. Parenting all children the same is like the "one-size-fits-all" concept. One size fits no one well! Knowing how your child is wired enables you to strengthen the skills that will maximize her or his talents. Having a plan to help your children obtain the best fit between themselves and the world can enhance their chances of success and happiness. That improves their resilience and is the fulfillment of the dream we all share for our children.

The *very* Not-so-easy Child (NSEC) exists, as any of the parents with one will tell you. Many family members and friends of parents with an NSEC give frequent well-meaning advice: "If you would just do this or that, you wouldn't have problems." Such edicts increase the guilt that these parents already have. This advice comes from adults who have not experienced an NSEC, but who have raised an easy child. Most anything will be successful in getting an easy child to behave, but the same tactic does not work with the child with at-risk temperament traits. Many parents of the NSEC have tried everything, resulting in minimal success and feelings of guilt because they think there is something wrong with themselves as parents.

Other children who have one or two of the hard to live with temperament traits sometimes fall into a gap between the easy and difficult levels. They will, at times, try your patience and sanity but at other times be easy. I have parents in my practice with children who have six, seven, or even eight at-risk temperament traits, and these children daily frustrate their parents, teachers, and caregivers. Bless these children's hearts. These at-risk, *very* Not-so-easy children are equally angry, frustrated, chronically bewildered, and overwhelmed. By age seven or eight, they commonly show signs of anxiety and emerging depression. They may begin to hit their heads with admonitions of being dumb, bad, or stupid for doing something that is upsetting the parent or teacher. This is often followed by compulsive behaviors and even tics, all attempts to calm their anxiety. Wouldn't you be anxious if you were in trouble all the time?

TANTRUMS, FITS, MELTDOWNS, AND MUDHOLE EXPERIENCES

When children are overwhelmed, frustrated, unable to express themselves, or expected to do something in conflict with their temperament, they may lock up or fall apart. They cannot solve the problem at hand. A wheel comes off! They go nuts. Adult tantrums or fits manifest as anger issues. So, if one parent has anger issues, it is a safe bet that at least one child will be NSE and vice versa. Many adults view childhood tantrums as manipulative in nature, blaming the child as only seeking to get her way or to get attention. The following discussion presents a strategy to determine the difference between tantrums for manipulation and temperament tantrums. Tantrums in which the child is attempting to get his way or to manipulate you tend to stop when attention is withdrawn. Tantrums caused by a conflict of expectation and the child's temperament do not stop when attention is stopped. If your child melts down for thirty minutes after you insist that she "Do it now!" that tantrum is due to a poor fit. The child cannot help it. The length of a meltdown can vary from five minutes to hours. Remember, when a child is melting down, leave her alone; trying to stop the meltdown only leads to her lashing out. Example: Devin is a very non-adaptive child and is locking up when prodded to do something without warning. Dad ignores the lockup—remember, this is the time to calm down and solve the problem—and instead yells, "Do it now!" Do it now is a phrase non-adaptive children cannot process. I refer to Do it Now as a Taser word. When used, it Tasers the child's frontal lobes and paralyses him. The child looks like he is resisting and being disrespectful, but he has just been Tased. The next step is that the child begins to melt down. He is overwhelmed and cannot solve dad's command and the brain shuts down. Dad continues to push, the child then lashes out with spitting, kicking, and name-calling, and the dad really gets mad and lashes out, leading to the mudhole.

Everyone exits the mudhole covered in mud. It represents a dysfunctional reaction to a poor fit expectation of the parent. If you insist on going into the mudhole with your child, if you try to extract him from the quagmire, you will succeed only in making the situation worse, and you both will soon be covered in mud. You will be angrier, more frustrated, and later will feel guilty that you acted that way. Do not push your child into the mudhole by attempting to stop a tantrum, crying jag, or wall-banging-yelling-lashing-out. This is an example of a parent-induced mudhole experience. Children can drive themselves to the mudhole. All in all, the mudhole is an experience to be avoided by knowing your child and how to handle lockups.

Earlier I spoke about the child with a hearing loss who has the responsibility to understand, regardless of his inability to hear. Children who are not easy fit into the same category with problem solving. They are responsible for solving the problem, but do not have the tools. When you insist that a non-adaptive child do something immediately, you have, in essence, yelled at a child with a hearing loss and expected her to hear. She cannot. That is the type of conflict causing most misbehavior. It is a mismatched expectation and an at-risk temperament trait. This is what I mean by behavior not being intentional, but rather that the child is so overwhelmed with the demand that he is unable to comply because the expectation conflicts with his temperament. We do not continue just to excuse the behavior, but we teach the child how to solve the problem that is attached to the temperament trait causing him to be overwhelmed. When a child is melting down, relax and let the child run out of gas. A child can also drive himself into the mudhole when something he plans does not work out. This can be as simple as the Cocoa Puffs example. After coaching your child to develop and strengthen skills that are weak, parents can manage these temperament traits and eliminate the meltdowns completely.

How Do You Handle Meltdowns Once Your Child Is Melting Down?

My academic clinical practice is combined with real-life experience of a very close relative who was a very Not-So-Easy Child. He is as sweet as any child and sweeter than most but had been known to have two-plus-hour mudhole meltdowns.

After learning processes, tips, and accepting help and these techniques that you are currently reading about, he has become a balanced, problem-solving, non-angry, calm young adult. He has learned how to manage his weaker skills with the help of his parents' persistent help that began when he was eight.

Although temperament changes little over time, positive change does occur when parents are diligently teaching their children how to overcome what overwhelms them. If parents strive to understand their children's temperament and alter their approach by teaching their children the skills that are weak and enhancing the strong ones, children will enter adulthood with a greater opportunity for success. The cautious or shy child can grow up with the ability to stand in front of large crowds and speak. The less adaptive child can learn to plan for the unexpected. One of my parent clients related that his child said, "I can really relax now when I have a backup plan for my backup plan." Parents have the opportunity to expand the capabilities of their children and ensure success for those children who are at-risk for struggles.

Over the past twenty years, there has been much research focused on these skills, particularly in early childhood development. My research team has completed a research study measuring executive functions in over a thousand prekindergarten students in a suburban school system. Our findings show that one-third of the children have significant at-risk executive functioning for inhibitory control, cognitive flexibility, emotional control, and working memory. The good news is EFs can be improved. There is current research worldwide addressing the development of interventions to improve executive functions in children. Executive-function training will be necessary to improve these children's skills the same as working with children with at-risk temperament traits. There is some overlap with temperament and executive functions measuring the same functions. If we look at only inhibitory control (impulse control), we know that there is some gradual natural improvement of physical impulse control over time, but the impulsiveness of a child's mind jumping from one thing to another, termed monkey brain, doesn't improve very much over time without specific training. The earlier the training starts, the more significant the improvement.

Everyone is familiar with ADHD. Most people understand some of the symptoms of ADHD, as viewed from the executive-function point of view. Symptoms of ADHD include poor inhibitory control and poor working memory. ADHD is primarily a learning disorder, not a behavioral one. Medicine prescribed for ADHD improves the impulse-control portion and does not improve working memory, and if the child has coexisting behavioral issues, the meds don't help those either. This diagnosis is currently made in approximately eight percent of the school population. The percentage jumps to thirty-plus percent of the early childhood population when the children's assessment includes an evaluation of their executive functions, impulse control, and working memory. We now know that executive functions predict school performance better than IQ. Executive functioning is now the basis for understanding what makes children learn and behave.

NOW YOU HAVE A SNAPSHOT OF THE TRAITS AND EXECUTIVE FUNCTIONS OF YOUR AND YOUR CHILD'S BRAIN. LET'S TALK ABOUT A MANAGEMENT PLAN.

STEP TWO: ASSURING SUCCESS– THE PLAN

CHAPTER 5

DESIGNING A MANAGEMENT PLAN FOR YOUR UNIQUE CHILD

Avoiding Meltdowns and Calls from Child Protective Services

A good management plan always starts with general guidelines and principles. After that section, we will discuss each of the temperament traits and executive functions and how you can improve the fit for each. Help Sheets in the Appendix go into more detail about each temperament trait.

GENERAL GUIDELINES

Here is your first parenting pearl:
Always give your child a warning of what you expect to happen next. **Use the words, "I expect you to"—whatever it is that you expect— "within the next (you select time) five, ten, fifteen minutes." Provide a reasonable timeframe for the task and a delay for the child's brain to catch up to what you are directing the child to do. The next step is to set a minute timer to your time expectation and to walk away.**

Most parents come back the next week after using the timer repeatedly and consistently report, "That timer is magic!"

A recent study showed that today's parents ask a child to do something using the same words three to five times. Then they repeat the request using different and stronger words another three to five times, and then most commonly the parent yells and threatens. The majority of the time, there is no following consequence. If you were a child, would you do what you are asked the first time? In telling the child what you expect and a timeframe in which to get it accomplished, it is the child's responsibility to comply or suffer the consequences. Constant micromanaging and telling children what to do rather than telling them what you expect them to accomplish is much less effective. This plan works for teenagers, especially teenagers who want to argue about everything. Stop nagging, arguing, threatening, reminding, and *expect your children to comply.* If they don't, administer a consequence. If this is done regularly and consistently, compliance will improve to meet your expectations (much more about consequences later).

Second parenting pearl: *Be patient.*

In parents' multitasking, rapid-pace, stress-filled world, your expectations are often unrealistic for your children. Young children are less prepared for rapid-fire commands. Their brains are still developing, their experience is limited, their problem-solving skills are incomplete, and often children need to borrow your fully developed brain to help them comply with all the things you ask of them.

Third parenting pearl: *Put yourself in their shoes.*

Haven't you wished your parents had walked a mile in your shoes? How many times have you suffered the consequences because you failed to understand exactly what was expected because clear expectations were not made and you didn't feel secure enough to clarify the request? Much of the time, we do not know what is going on in our child's head, the stresses she feels, or whether she understands what we mean when we *tell her* to do something. Most children, most of the time, want to please us and carry out what we ask them to do. Do not do it for them, but help them develop the skills to complete their responsibility.

Fourth parenting pearl: *Shift into Emotional Neutral.*

Most of the time, when parents get frustrated and angry, it's because they are not solving the current problem with their child very well. First, let's talk about why getting angry is counterproductive. When we are angry, we shift the child's focus from solving the problem we gave them to keeping us from being angry. We have added another layer to the problem that can cause long-term issues in interpersonal relationships. Many times, we get angry because we ask repeatedly, and the child doesn't do what we expect or doesn't do it fast enough. We spoke earlier about having no consequences if the child doesn't follow through and comply with our wishes. When I ask parents about how they discipline, most of them generally talk about all the ways they don't discipline. Many parents relate that they discipline as the *last resort* and not as they should, as the *first resort*. Most parents first try to explain, re-explain, argue, nag, or threaten. These are not consequences. When this is not successful, they yell, scream, and punish.

What is meant by consequences?

The consequence principle is the natural result of an action or inaction. If a pupil misses questions on a test or fails to turn in his homework, a poor grade results, a natural consequence. If you don't do your work, your boss will likely give you a consequence, a dressing down, a write-up or, for chronic failure to comply with requests, the resultant loss of a job. If you run a red light, you may get a ticket. The teacher or boss doesn't yell or scream or threaten you. They just dole out the consequence. The policeman doesn't walk up and bang on your window demanding why you ran a red light; he just writes you a ticket (consequence). Dispensing consequences to our children should be unemotional. Some parents confuse a consequence with punishment. Punishment generally is what happens after we get angry. Giving consequences or disciplining is what should happen when a child fails to comply with what we expect, and it is done in a calm, unemotional way.

Consequences are small and frequent. If it is large and infrequent, it is punishment and does not teach—it only makes the child angry. A consequence is small and frequent and should just bug them. They get tired of having their day interrupted and will avoid these same issues in the future. Be kind and empathetic, not angry. Keep telling yourself that your child is overwhelmed and not just being defiant. Remember, any anger will only become your child's focus, and it usually forces the child into the mudhole. Anger is a manipulative tool parents use to make the child obey or feel guilty that they have not pleased the parent. Don't go there—it is a dysfunctional parenting action. Remain calm; you are the adult, and you need to lend your child some of your higher-brain-function problem-solving. (See Consequences in the Help Sheet section.)

> *Do not attempt to increase the power or manipulate with a promise of rewards or punishments. State the obvious: you are locked up, overwhelmed, etc.*

HOW TO GO FROM LOCKUP TO PROBLEM SOLVED

(The complete steps for problem-solving are found in the Appendix Help Sheets, under "Help Sheet #1, Getting to Now What.")

- **Step one.** ***Get everyone calm.*** This may require the exercise of slowly blowing out her/his imaginary birthday candles. This slow exhalation of breath has a natural calming effect. Breathing fast has the opposite effect. After your child is calm, ask your child, "What is wrong?" Really listen to the answer. The biggest complaint children have about their parents is that they do not listen. When you listen, and repeat what was said, the first step in solving the problem is accomplished. Everyone is clear about what the problem is. If the child has trouble stating what is wrong, you may state what you identify as the problem. "I know you don't like surprises," or, "I know you are hungry."

- **Step two.** ***Be reassuring with the child:*** "I know you are upset, but it will be all right. Now let's solve this problem." You have now shifted from what was an emotional reaction to a problem-solving exercise that is not emotional. As we have said earlier, when you are emotional, you lose IQ points and are unable to solve the problem. When you are calm, you not only prevent the meltdown, but you teach your child the valuable skill of problem-solving. Children four years and older may prefer first to spend some quiet time to calm themselves down and then start the problem-solving exercise. This may seem like it takes a lot of time, but eventually it takes less time, energy, and certainly causes less stress.
- What if by the time you realize your child has locked up, they are melting down? Wait out the meltdown calmly. Never punish a child for a meltdown; that is like punishing a child for having a seizure. They are both involuntary and a natural neurologic progression of a wiring problem.
- **Step three.** ***Address the problem and possible solutions only after the child has calmed down.***

After living with our own children for years and experiencing their reactions, my wife and I began to alter our approach. Here is one lesson I learned: When on vacation, despite my desire to drive for two hours straight while our highly active children were young, I learned, with much encouragement from my wife, to alter that course and stop every forty-five minutes. Our change of pace allowed the children to do jumping jacks in a roadside park for five minutes. Such a quick hiatus helped to dispel the pent-up energy of the children and substituted peace in the backseat for sibling conflict or another disruptive crisis. Even pediatricians learn parenting by trial and error. Tailoring our expectations does cause improvement in subsequent behavior from children. My wife intuitively negotiated a good plan to help us handle my unrealistic expectation of nonstop travel and our children's high-activity temperament traits.

When anger erupts because of the frustration arising from conflicting parental needs and children's lack of self-control, we as parents need to teach our sons and daughters some of our self-restraint by anticipating disagreements and altering our expectations. Changing these expectations is not actually giving in to our children. I do not believe, as I have said before, that, "My temperament made me do it." All children, NSE or not, are responsible for their actions and behavior, but we as parents should not push them into the mudhole and then punish them; this would be very unfair and unreasonable when we are the cause of the meltdown. The guidance of an understanding parent can decrease meltdowns dramatically. Remember, child's negative actions are not intentional, but merely the result of being overwhelmed with the current problem he or she cannot solve.

There are approaches to lessen your difficulties and improve the ways to parent children with at-risk or hard-to-live-with aspects of temperament. What follows are strategies to manage each specific temperament trait. (See the parental help sheets in the back of the book for additional tips.)

Here is the management plan for the not-so-easy child with at-risk temperament traits.

Soon after I established my parent-focused practice, a new patient called to make an appointment for help with her nine-year-old son. During the first session with the mother and father, one of the major problems was established to be meltdowns. Their evenings were a constant source of frustration. When I asked, "What is the best you can hope for most evenings?" The reply was, "Thirty minutes of complaining and sulking and the worst is an hour-plus meltdown." The father admitted that he was a "Do it Now!" type of dad. The "Do it Now!" type of parent frequently yells at the child, "Stop doing what you're doing, and do this now. I said now, right now!" I suggested, "Why don't you tell your son what you expect and give him a period in which to accomplish it?" As in, "Son, I expect you to go take your shower within the next five minutes." My instructions continued for him to do this calmly and without emotion in his voice. The result was a skeptical glance, but the father promised to try it. The next morning the telephone rang. It was the father, who said, "Well, let me tell you what happened last night. I really did not think this would work because you don't really know my son, but I tried it your way. Last night our son had finished his homework and was allowed to watch a little TV. It became time for him to shower, and I almost did as I usually do and yelled to him, Go take your shower now! Stop what you are doing right now and get upstairs and take your shower. Instead, I remembered what you said, shifted into emotional neutral, and calmly said, Son, after the next commercial, it will be time to shower. To my amazement, after the commercial, he got up, turned off the TV, and went to take his shower. We did not have a fight last night. I didn't think that simple a solution would work, but it did."

Understanding your child's temperament wiring and not expecting something that conflicts with those traits is not rocket science. Understanding is the necessary first step in developing a plan to help your child strengthen those skill sets that are not strong and enhancing those that are.

TEMPERAMENT TRAITS

Behavior Drivers

Adaptability/Non-adaptability (High/low tolerance for frustration)

A *slowly* adaptable child exhibits slowness to change behavior in meeting the expectations of others. These children are truly the "no surprises" kids. They do not respond well to a command of, "Do it Now!" They have a slower processing speed and require more time to respond to a request. These youngsters may have difficulty altering their usual reactions and require more time to adjust. "Sink or swim" approaches may lead to more difficulties for this child. She will also have more frustration and a lower tolerance for frustration than average, which can lead to locked-up behavior often called resistance and defiance, and which appears to be "disrespect." She will first shut down as she becomes overwhelmed with the request to change, and then melt down if pushed, and lash out if continued pressure to conform is demanded. Her slow process speed makes advanced warning and time to change a necessity. These children are planners, always asking what will happen next. They realize they do not solve problems quickly and need to plan how they are going to respond. Not knowing what is going to happen is a constant source of anxiety for these children. If they do not learn to calm themselves, they will begin to do things repetitively, called obsessive-compulsive behavior, in order to calm themselves. This commonly manifests in bedtime routines that must be accomplished in the same order and if interrupted requires the process to repeat. This leads to long-term anxiety, which then leads to depression. Therefore, it is vitally important to help these children suffering from the non-adaptable temperament trait.

These children do not choose nor plan to behave as they do when temperament and expectations conflict. The child is not intentionally disobeying, being resistant, or defiant.

A slowly adaptable child has real difficulty with changes in plans, requests to shift gears, and in accommodating the demands of others. It is your job as a parent to help the child stay calm while solving a problem and to give her time to solve that problem. The more advanced warning the child receives, the calmer she becomes. If you have a child like this, now you know why time is important, why she is always asking what will happen next, and where her important people will be.

Children who are resistant to change also have a low tolerance for frustration. This difficulty includes all cognitive skills of higher executive functioning:

- Shifting from one mindset to another (from play to work, from wake to sleep, or from sleep to wake)
- Developing a coherent plan to deal with the problem or frustration
- Performing multiple thinking tasks at once

- Being able to go from an emotional response to a problem-solving thinking response

These children need help in learning how to:

- *Recognize* feelings as she/he is beginning to get frustrated
- *Unlock* his usual locked-in behavior
- *Think* to solve her current problem
- *Negotiate* a solution to *this situation*

The first thing is to understand that these children cannot help this reaction of response. The next thing is to accept that he needs help to develop some skills to cope with his temperament. "My temperament made me do it" is ***not*** an acceptable excuse for behavior, and he is responsible for the outcome. Empathy is warranted and anger at your child's reaction is not appropriate. A well-planned structure and consequence program (Laws, Rules and SOPs: see later chapter) needs to be in place while changes are made and you as parents take over management of the family with a new understanding of what makes your child tick.

Highly adaptable children, on the other hand, need to be encouraged to question what people are asking them to do. The children who tend to go along with all instructions may have no trouble keeping friends, but peers can put them at risk by inducing them to ignore good judgment. Your job with these children is to teach them to problem-solve and not just go along with the situation. This needs to be done sooner rather than later, so that when it is suggested to your fifteen-year-old daughter by her new boyfriend, "Let's take off our clothes and smoke this," she will not just go along to please.

Approach/withdrawal or curious/cautious

Withdrawal temperament indicates a reluctance to experience new or unfamiliar situations or circumstances. Most people just call this *cautious* or shy or "she just needs a little warm-up time." With time, many of these initially rejected activities may become tolerated or even desired. New things should be introduced slowly and in small amounts. Pushing and insisting that a withdrawing child try something new may frighten him and set up a pattern of avoidance. A gradual introduction can lead to acceptance and maybe even bring enjoyment. Explaining new things in advance will be very helpful. An example of gradual exposure would be how to introduce peas to a child. When today's parents introduce a new food, they put it on the plate, followed by much encouragement. If the child refuses, the peas are shelved for a while. This ensures that at each new introduction, the child views the peas as a new food. If you have a cautious child, the response will always be the same: "No." Instead, put the peas on the child's plate every day for a week. The first night, say nothing; the child observes and may remark or ignore them. The next night, calmly instruct and demonstrate by touching a pea. That is all—just touch one. The next night, smell one; the next night, lick one; and the next night, taste it. By this time, the pea is no longer new, and the child will judge the pea as a pea, and not as something new.

For the older child, an example would be trying a new restaurant. You know that your cautious child will resist and prefer to go to the restaurant you usually frequent. When you introduce this without a gradual introduction, the result may be having a fit in the entry while waiting on the table. How do you introduce a new restaurant to a reluctant-to-try child?

First, as you drive by that restaurant one day, say, "Dad and I want to try that restaurant one of these days." The next time you drive past the new restaurant, say, "I'm going to drive in closer to see what the restaurant looks like." The next time, you say, "We have a few minutes; let's just stop and go inside and see what it looks like, smells like, and look at the menu." Most restaurants have their own website, which makes this restaurant introduction to your child a gradual virtual tour and review of the menu. Most of the time, when parents try this approach, there is less resistance to trying it the first time. It takes withdrawing children some time to get used to something new.

With this example, you are teaching a valuable lesson to your child of how to overcome his initial resistance to something new. You already know if you ask your child to try something new to please you, it rarely works.

As this *cautious* child matures, he will continue to be very cautious and reluctant to participate in new activities, but now he has a skill to overcome this inborn trait. This temperament trait will lead to careful picking of friends who have a similar approach to life and avoidance of the riskier, chance-taking behaviors. This trait is protective; these children would rarely go off with a stranger.

On the other hand, the *very curious* or *approaching* child loves something new just because it is new. These children are the risk-takers, and because of that are at risk to go off with a stranger, jump off the roof, and many other things that you never thought could happen. My wife and I had one of each: one cautious and one curious. As an example, the curious one did not want training wheels on the new bike but preferred to learn how to ride by falling. The second child was cautious and did not want the training wheels removed. Which child do you think had been in the emergency room numerous times, and which one had never been in one?

Sensory Threshold

- Children with the *low* sensory threshold, or the highly sensitive child, represent their own set of challenges. These children easily become overwhelmed when something is too tight, too loud, too bright, or too scratchy. If the room is too hot, too cold, or just smelly, it can overwhelm them, lock them up, and cause a meltdown. Books have been written on this subject: *Too Loud, Too Bright, Too Fast, Too Tight,* by Sharon Heller, PhD, and The Highly Sensitive Child by Elaine Aron, PhD.

- You can help the sensitive child by labeling behavior, "I know you don't like tight clothes but..." This transmits compassion but with the expectation that the child will still be responsible for her actions. A common "parent-child poor fit" is between the low-sensory-threshold child and the parent with a normal or high sensory threshold. The parent who has never felt this way may overlook this highly sensitive child's response to tight clothing. This conflict is played out in a story related by one of my parents about her child. This mother had three children, only one of whom had a low sensory threshold. Mother had a normal sensory threshold and was very practical. When it became extremely cold outside, she thought the appropriate dress was a turtleneck wool sweater. Her daughter's reaction was a constant clawing at her neck and whining about the turtleneck being too tight and too scratchy. The other two children were perfectly fine with their required dress, so mom thought her sensitive child was just being difficult. After a temperament assessment on her child, she then understood why her daughter refused and melted down when she brought out the turtleneck sweater on cold days. She understands her daughter cannot stand wool material tight against her neck, regardless of how warm it feels. The mother related that when she told her child that they would send all her turtlenecks to a cousin and she would not make her wear turtlenecks when it was cold, the child replied, "Oh, Mama, I love you so much." What may seem like a minor thing—little steps to some parents—means a great deal to children who are very sensitive.

- Another parent related the story of their son with a low sensory threshold who recently had tried on thirteen pairs of shoes searching for that special pair that "felt right." Children who are sensitive are ruled by sensory stimulation and must eliminate all overloading input to be able to function. Be patient with these sensitive children who cannot help their reactions.

The *high* sensory threshold or less sensitive children have decreased sensitivity to sounds, lights, colors, textures, temperature, pain, tastes, smells, dirt, etc.

They have:

- Minor interest in the taste of food and are unbothered by spicy foods.
- Under-reaction to pain, such as minor cuts and scrapes.

- Less appreciation of temperature changes, loud noises, and confusion.
- Less empathy for others.
- Less awareness of others' space and presence.
- Less awareness of nonverbal social cues.
- Less awareness of implied social messages.

These children need higher levels of sensory input before changes in their behavior are seen. Repetition is needed for them to learn socially accepted responses. Their pain threshold is high, so attention should be paid to any distress from pain. They often need social clues explained and reiterated. They may need a failed social relationship or social expectation explained in more detail. You can help them by stating:

- "I know that it is difficult for you to respect others' space. You like to stay very close, but most of your friends like their eighteen-inch bubble around them."
- "I know it is hard for you to understand what others are experiencing."
- "I know it does not bother you when someone does that, but it does bother your friend."

They may seek increased sensory stimulation, such as louder noises, etc., and you may have to speak louder to get their attention. Repetition is needed to learn rules and socially accepted responses, respect for personal space, and for others' feelings. (See the help pages in the Appendix for more help with children with high sensory thresholds.)

Here are some social skills that all children need to master, but are not easily learned by the less sensitive

- Listening to others
- Understanding that others' points of view are important

- Conversing
- Asking what others mean, feel, or want
- Convincing others
- Knowing their feelings
- Expressing their feelings
- Recognizing and expressing empathy
- Negotiating compromises
- Conflict resolution

Body Clock Regularity

- **Irregularity** requires parents to understand that rigid schedules and obsession about routines will be a less than optimal parenting technique for these children. Having regular mealtimes and social interchange is great but expecting a child who is not hungry to eat at a regular mealtime is unrealistic. Separate eating and mealtime by allowing protein or vegetable or fruit snacks up until one-and-a-half-hours before and after meals. You may use the same approach of separating bedtime from sleep time. Bedtime may be at 8:00 p.m. but sleep only comes when a child is sleepy; allow quiet time (underline quiet) for a thirty-minute period before the lights go out. Children today do not have enough alone or quiet time to reflect, plan, and let their minds wander and play. They may remain awake for a while after lights go out, but you can adjust your expectations to be in accord with their temperament traits of irregularity. Very regular children may get hungry and sleepy within a short period every day and become cranky when not allowed to fulfill these needs. Plan ahead. Carry snacks and add rest times to the day that will be a long one and when the eating and rest schedule will be interrupted.

Trait Modifiers

- The intensity of a child does not drive behavior but modifies it. It is their volume control. Highly intense children talk loudly and cry very loudly, but they also laugh with contagious, noisy pleasure. They live life with gusto. Nothing with these children can be ignored; everybody knows what is going on. The mildly intense child speaks softly, reacts mildly, and generally would be considered a quiet child. These children often have needs that are unmet because of this temperament trait. These are the children to pay more attention to because when they speak, it is important to pay more attention.

Mood

- Is your child's glass "half full" or "half empty?" Do they take things very seriously that are not serious? How your children react to the situation is not an indication of whether they are happy or not. It is merely their first reaction to the situation. One of my parents contrasted his two children—one very positive and the other negative—with this story. They had just completed an amusement ride at the fair and the positive child was saying, "Man, that was awesome," and the negative child responded, "Well that wasn't as bad as I thought it was going to be." They obviously both enjoyed the ride, but their responses reflected their mood temperament trait. Negative-mood children have a half empty set point that makes them hard to live with sometimes, but it is not your fault, and they still love you regardless of their mood. Tell yourself that this is just the way they are and that they cannot help it. Attempting to reverse the negativity usually makes things worse: "Oh, it isn't that bad" is met with, "Is too!" This unnecessary conflict becomes frustrating for both parent and child. Being negative is one of those traits that everyone must learn to live with, and the child will change as she experiences the fact that most people do not always appreciate a contrary, complaining attitude. There is a positive side to this trait in that planning teams need someone to present challenges such as, "That's not going to work!" This causes everyone to reevaluate a situation in more detail. Being negative, to a degree, can characterize a valuable person on any team, since the very positive team member sometimes ignores reality with his always-positive attitude. When a positive parent and a negative child see the same problem in very different lenses it often results in conflict, but it doesn't have to if you recognize your own temperament. Knowing yourself as a parent is as important as knowing your child's temperament.

Learning Drivers

High activity high energy level children require plenty of opportunities to be active. Do not plan long periods of inactivity without exercise, or you are asking for crises, tantrums, meltdowns, and mudhole experiences. Exercise in the mall before you require them to stand still and "not touch anything" in the store. Parents can help their children understand their high energy by labeling the behavior before it leads to problems: "You are beginning to get restless, overexcited, and wild; it is time to go outside and run." On the other end of the scale, the low-activity or low-energy child needs to be encouraged to exercise because the major risk factor over time is obesity.

Persistence

- The *highly* persistent child needs a preemptive reminder: "I know you are focused and don't want to stop but..." or, "It is hard for you not to finish, but sometimes it is all right to finish later." The persistent child will make you proud by not giving up when you want her to do something and will drive you to insanity by refusing to give up when you want her to. You cannot have it both ways. Stubbornness is a trait that can help a child be successful. I got a call from a frantic parent in the fall soon after school started. Her four-year-old boy had just been expelled from pre-K for being violent. In tears, the mother assured me that her child was anything but aggressive and was very kind and would not hurt anyone. Could I please help? A Temperament Assessment revealed a child who was sensitive and very persistent but with no other at-risk traits. Neither of these traits would usually be connected to aggressive behavior. I called the school and was told the following story about the incidents that led to this boy's expulsion.
- The kindergarten classes had a fair in the gym. There was food and fun, with activity stations around the floor. This child, let's call him Bryan, entered the gym and stopped abruptly after only a few feet, and began to crouch down and refused to move any farther. The teacher rather forcefully had to pull Bryan to the first activity station and then spend ten minutes calming him down. Finally, he calmed and began the project represented in the booth. He became engrossed and was "really into it" when it was time to move on. The teacher announced that it was time to move, but Bryan refused, still working on his project; he had not finished. The teacher

then began to forcefully push him to stop the project and move on. He refused, the teacher pushed more, Bryan melted down, and the teacher tried to forcefully move Bryan. Just then a girl passed by, and Bryan lashed out and pushed the little girl. She fell and hit her head, seemed stunned, and complained of a headache. Her mother, who was volunteering at the fair, ran over, scooped her daughter up, and rushed her to their doctor. This scared the school administrators, and they decided that Bryan was too aggressive for their pre-K program and expelled him.

- How do we explain what was going on with Bryan and the incident in the gym? His temperament traits were assessed as being sensitive, and when this sensitive four-year-old was introduced to the gym experience of smells and chaotic confusion, he balked. He was overwhelmed with the noise, smells, movement, and confusion. He almost melted down but regained his composure and began his project. He also tested as very persistent, and typically, when a child is persistent and is not allowed to finish his project, he locks up. The teacher did not give any warning of the change, nor did she explain that he could finish his project later. Bryan locked up. The teacher continued to push, and the teacher pushed him into the mudhole, and he melted down. She continued to insist and push and he lashed out. The typical behavior of all children with this temperament profile when pushed beyond their limits is to lock up, melt down, and lash out if not helped to resolve the lockup. He is not an aggressive child, but he reacted in a fashion expected for his temperament traits in the situation. The teacher didn't understand him and caused him to lash out, accidentally hurting the little girl. After a conference with the principal and the teacher, they better understood what the causative factors were and reinstated him.

- The *less persistent* child needs encouragement to stay focused and on-task through statements such as, "Why don't you take a short break, and you can get right back to this after a break." These "give-up-easily" children are often labeled as lazy, but they are not persistent when there are things they do not want to do. (See the Help Sheet #5 in the back of the book.)
- *Highly distractible* children need a persistent parent to refocus direction frequently and kindly: "Whoops, you've lost your place; you were going to bring me the book, weren't you?" After gaining the child's attention with, "Look at my eyes," it's wise to break down directions into, "First, you do this; second, you do that." Providing specific instructions increases success. Parents with a child who has trouble focusing will be pleased to learn that creativity frequently comes from this type of active mind.
- Einstein probably drove his mother crazy! (See Help Sheet #5)

As **temperamental** *misbehavior* begins, you may feel your anger rising; it is best to stop and take a slow, long exhalation breath. Then *think*, "Is this due to temperament?" This approach eliminates the parental knee-jerk reaction to perceived misbehavior and permits objectivity to occur. A calm response reduces the kind of upheaval that makes everyone's day unhappy, stressful, and nonproductive.

Each trait is discussed separately, but, of course, they do not occur that way. Children who are persistent may also be negative and resist change or be positive and adaptable. The combination makes each child unique and is the reason one-size parenting advice doesn't fit all. We have established that all children are different. We know each child is unique, but it is still common for the parenting experts to espouse "One way fits all" for managing a child. How can that be effective if all children are different? *Knowing your child's temperament is essential for effective parenting.* What is required to gain an "easy" child's attention is very different from summoning up the energy to get the attention of a not-so-easy-child. To attempt to treat all your children the same is a formula for problems. Your children will immediately see that you have a different approach to each of them and may cry foul, but unless you individualize the approach to your children, they may feel that you are unfair to all of them. *Always keep in mind that the individual approach is the key to good parenting. Being fair by treating all children the same is a recipe for problems.*

EXECUTIVE DYSFUNCTION AND A MANAGEMENT PLAN

Executive functions are the cognitive abilities that control and regulate most of what we do in everyday life. Executive functions include the ability to start a process, plan and organize, set goals, solve problems, regulate emotions, and monitor behavior. These skills play a role in everything we do. Executive Function deficits can hamper a child behaviorally, academically, and socially. They are present from an early age, and problems with executive functions begin as early as three years old. We have known that children with superior executive functions (EF) do better in reading and math in school. My colleagues and I have just completed a research project assessing all 1,100 pre-K students in a suburban school district and found that poor EF skills predicted behavioral and learning problems. In children as young as four years of age, we see how important these skills are to success in the school setting. My practice of almost fifteen years has certainly confirmed the difficulty and problems that poor EF skills cause at home and at school. These EF skills are listed as: impulse control (inhibitory control), controlling emotions and social behaviors, abstract reasoning or concept formation (cognitive flexibility), task initiation, working memory, planning, organization and time management, organization of materials, self-monitoring, and regulation. Expansion of these categories is as follows:

Behavioral

a. **Inhibition** - The ability to stop one's own behavior at the appropriate time, including stopping actions and thoughts. The flip side of inhibition is impulsivity; if you have weak ability to stop yourself from acting on your impulses, then you are "impulsive."
b. **Shift** - The ability to move freely from one situation to another and to think flexibly in order to respond appropriately to the situation. This, in temperament trait expression, is equal to the adaptability trait.
c. **Emotional Control** - The ability to modulate emotional responses by bringing rational thought to bear on feelings.

Educational/learning

Working memory (WM) - The capacity to hold information in mind for the purpose of completing a task. WM is broken down into these components:

1. **Initiation** - The ability to begin a task or activity and to independently generate ideas, responses, or problem-solving strategies.
2. **Planning/Organization/Time Management** - The ability to manage current and future-oriented task demands and time constraints.
3. **Organization of Materials** - The ability to impose order on work, play, and storage spaces.
4. **Self-Monitoring** - The ability to monitor one's own performance and to measure it against some standard of what is needed or expected.

Common diagnoses of poor executive function skills or executive dysfunction as it is called include ADHD, Oppositional Defiant Disorder (ODD), and anxiety, to name just a few. ADHD is difficulty with impulse control and working memory. ODD is non-adaptive behavior. Temperament and EF traits are the symptoms of the diagnosis, which represent the composite of symptoms.

I spoke in an earlier chapter about how to help and manage impulse control. The other modality is drug therapy. ADHD drugs only help the impulse-control portion of ADHD, but do not help the working memory part. The only known things proven to help the WM portion are three things: meditation, tae kwon do, and a licensed computer program called Cogmed. (www.cogmed.com) Cognitive therapy with a licensed psychologist or therapist can also help with the behavioral issues discussed.

CHAPTER 6

CREATING THE ENVIRONMENT: FAMILY GUIDELINES

Changing "Dysfunctions Are Us" to "*Wow* that Works"

What would happen if all the air-traffic controllers walked off their jobs at the same time? What would happen if everyone wanted service at once and ignored the standard courtesy to line up? What would happen if all people could take whatever they wanted, whenever they wanted it, and from anyone they wanted?

Chaos and anger are my first two thoughts—that, or a three-year-old daycare class. Guidelines are an absolute necessity for life's structure and therefore every family's structure.

It is up to you, the parent, to establish a consistent and defined structure to your children's lives. Successfully teaching your children requires a set of guidelines that ideally both parents agree on and your children know and understand. When you set up these guidelines, you are creating a rehearsal hall for real life. You as an adult lead your life by laws, rules, and standard expectations for living with others, while maintaining peace. Your kids need the same boundaries. They only feel safe and secure when they know what to expect.

When they make their first mistakes in this early environment, and you know they *will*, the costs are minimal. If you try to prevent those early mistakes or protect them from the consequences when they are young, the mistakes made later always have more severe outcomes. This delay in learning a lesson can cause life-restricting results. Guidelines are an essential fact of life.

Assure your children that you love them by establishing guidelines. When parents don't set boundaries, children become more insistent to find the boundary. Why? They are really seeking validation of your love! They know that rules and boundaries mean you are protecting them, that you love them. They remember that early in their lives, when you warned them of a danger and they didn't pay attention to the warning, they were injured. They tested your limits and you were right: they got hurt. You must love them and want to protect them. Rules do signify love.

Every child requires someone who is more stable, capable, stronger, and smarter. Your children need a model: you. If your children have a role model who lacks the strength to set guidelines, they will always be seeking, pushing, tugging, whining, arguing, testing, testing, and testing. They are searching for what is really expected of them and for written guidelines that will allow them to relax in the knowledge that you love them enough to establish parameters for their safety and well-being. With a written, posted set of guidelines, you as parents can also relax. No more making up rules on the fly that are changed the next week or the next day by another parent. You don't have to think, "What would my mate do in this circumstance?" or the frequent, "What do I do now?" Consistency will be an easy-to-follow concept when it is written. Insufficient limits or changing limits confuse and lead to unruly, unhappy, and demanding children. Children who have slow adaptable or inflexible temperaments need *very* firm boundaries and a structure that they can count on so they can feel secure. They react negatively when expectations change and boundaries are not firm. Your children will thrive only when they know exactly what is expected of them. They are robbed of this security and confidence when you don't set limits and consistently see that they are followed. Moving back to the work analogy: How would you feel if your boss changed the rules from week to week? Establishing guidelines sounds like a lot of trouble and time to compose, but I have a format and suggestions that make it easy. These have been honed over the years and have proven to be fair, succinct, commonsense, and broad enough to apply to every circumstance that you could possibly think of, fear, or imagine. Previous generations of curious children have solved that for you.

Do you repeat yourself, argue, and constantly explain your actions to your child? Do you nag and threaten your child to get a task done, only to fail to follow up on the threat? Are you often at a loss to know when to stand firm or be lenient? Do you often give in to your child's demands? How often do you flip-flop about being lenient or strict? If you answered yes to these questions, your children need for you to focus on improving the structure and consistency of your discipline.

You can put that structure into your family with Dr. Bob's Family By-Laws: The Concept of Laws, Rules, and SOPs (standard operating procedures).

Guidelines vary in importance, consequence, and outcome. **Laws** are the most important and deal with your children's safety. The consequence of breaking a law is the most severe, swift, and with no options for plea-bargains. **Rules** relate to personal privileges and property rights, and the consequence for an infraction is the removal of a privilege or a property. **SOPs** are defined as personal responsibilities, family operations (chores), and social conventions. "Say please, thank you, shake hands, and don't pick your nose in public." Removing pleasures and imposing fines deal with these infractions. These guidelines parallel our social structure in severity and consequences and are preparing your children for the real world. They mirror capital crime, felonies, and misdemeanors.

Why it is necessary to write it down? If you don't write it down, it isn't real! What is the difference in your response to your boss, colleague, friend, or mate saying, "I need you to do this," as opposed to receiving a note, text, email, or telegram that states, "I need you to do this?" If it is written, it is serious. So, spend a little time—it's only a one-time thing—to review the enclosed template for Laws, Rules, and SOPs. Edit them to suit your family's needs and post them on the family bulletin board. Have the children read and sign them. If they can't read, then spend a Saturday and take pictures of your children breaking the law, circle it with a sharpie, cross through it, and place the consequence next to the picture of the broken law. That visual leaves no doubt in your child's mind as to the law, expectation, and consequence. My parents say it was fun for them and their kids to put these guidelines together and that their understanding was amplified and their forgetting eliminated. When the child breaks a law, you only need to point to the infraction posted and not yell and rant about it. It also excludes the daily arguing so common when guidelines are not set.

When you set the penalty for choosing not to follow the guideline *before it is broken,* you don't have to think of the penalty on the spot and possibly make it stronger or weaker than is required. Pre-thought-out consequences that are agreed to by both parents lessen the age-old "you were too harsh or too lenient" parental infighting. That is a counterproductive parenting technique. When the consequence is pre-established with neither argument nor anger, it becomes a fact. Announce the guidelines, the consequences, and enforce those one-hundred percent with NO EXCEPTIONS. As I have emphasized before, children learn best from small, frequent consequences, not from infrequent, large, harsh, "lose your temper" consequences.

Discipline is the enforcement of consequences. Discipline is teaching. I have stressed this before, but it is important: *Do not confuse discipline with punishment. Discipline is teaching the natural consequences of choices and actions.* There are both positive and negative consequences of actions. In today's world let's define punishment as severe harm inflicted on a child after the parents have lost their temper. I don't believe in punishment, but have an absolute belief in the need for discipline in parenting. Discipline is an entrenched, expert-recognized, necessary principle of child-rearing. Children learn life's lessons from consequences. Punishments, on the other hand, just anger them and they learn nothing except punishment is "mean."

Discipline requires that you have your children's attention before they can learn the lesson. Sometimes this attention getting only requires a look to the "easy" child, but for the NSEC it requires more, such as your gently turning his/her face to yours for eye contact. Many children think if they don't make eye contact, they are not responsible for listening! Encourage listening. Explanations are okay but are not necessary. Overexplaining is counterproductive. A recent passing psychological fad was to explain everything to your children. That isn't necessary. Kids are not dumb, and after the same infraction has a consequence, they figure it out. Many children ask, "Why?" They ask, "Why" not to receive an answer, but to delay you from administering the consequences to their behavior. Don't fall into that trap. Follow through with the consequence without emotion. I am repeating this because it is vital. **Parental Rule:** Do not get "mad!" Your child becomes frightened at your anger and responds with fear. Fear of the loss of you and at the loss of love, and that results in missing the lesson of applied consequences. The less emotion that enters discipline, the more your child learns, and the less manipulation occurs. You can *make* your children mind you (*manipulate your child*) with many tricks, such as making them feel guilty and fearful of your anger or power, or by withdrawing love, but the important lessons are missed. The missed lesson will eventually have to be learned, often with more serious consequences. Make the best choice the first time around. When you run a stop sign and the policeman pulls you over, does he take you to jail? No. Does he pound on your roof, yell at you for running the stop sign, and ask you, "Why did you run that stop?" No. He just writes you a ticket.

Pre-established, consistent, and firmly enforced guidelines will make your family run more smoothly, make your parenting easier, and make your children feel secure that you care and love them. They won't worry that you don't love them, cringe that you are mad at them, or try to deny that they broke the rule. Your child tested the rule, got caught, and served the consequence. That unemotional response alone calms the household, and everyone has more energy and less anxiety at the end of the day.

CHAPTER 7

WHOSE PROBLEMS ARE THESE ANYWAY?

The 3 C's: Choices, Consistency, Consequences

How much should parents do for their child? In today's world, it seems like the answer is *everything*. Obviously, it is not everything, so how do you know if you are currently doing too much for your child? Current research and questionnaires show us that over-parenting, in all its forms, is becoming too common and the results are easily recognized in our teens and twenty-something young adults. They show disturbingly high rates of substance use, depression, anxiety, eating disorders, cheating, and stealing.

Are You a Helicopter, Lawnmower, or Overprotective Parent? Take the Quiz in the appendix Help Sheet # 7.
When you complete the quiz and have the score you will know the extent of your over parenting and this chapter will

be a better guide to help you let go of some child growth restraining habits.

Suggestions to Help Your Children Begin to Take Responsibility for Their Problems

Many children want help when they are confronted with a problem; you have been their "go-to guy" for solving the problem. It is time to stop. You are depriving your children of the opportunity to expand their database of skills by learning to solve their own problems. When your child yells, calls for help, or otherwise interrupts with an urgent plea, your first response will be to ask yourself, "Whose problem is this anyway?" Usually it is theirs—do not interfere by coming to the rescue.

These questions will expand your children's thinking possibilities. First, they must take ownership of their problems. This change will be new for both of you. The old way is for you to direct them. The new way is for you to give them the problem. This first step toward autonomy needs a new set of responses from you and a new set of questions for you to ask.

Here are some suggestions:

- "It seems you have a problem."
- "That doesn't seem to be working."
- "Maybe you should try something different."
- "What have you tried?"
- "I think you should give some thought to that."
- "In my experience, that's a difficult problem."
- "Whose idea was that?" Followed by, "Is that what you think?"
- "Does your friend's answer have to match yours?"
- "Can you disagree and still be okay?"

Each of the above is followed by ***silence*** until your child responds, then you ask other questions such as:

- "Could you have chosen a different way to approach or solve that?"
- "What are your options?"
- "What are some of the things you could try?" Then more silence.

A nice end to the discussion could be: "I'll be eager to see how you solve it." Encouragement is supportive: "I'm confident you can come up with a plan." Always lead them to the possibilities and not to *your* answers. This change is not easy for you or your child and is very different than your comfortable "giving directions," but I *am* confident that you will succeed!

Getting to Now What in the Appendix help sheets is a problem-solving process to follow for teaching your child when s/he is stuck. The best help parents can give their children is to serve as a base of reality, not as an encyclopedia of directions. Be easily accessible, not constantly present.

Choices, Choices, and More Choices

The following is an email I recently received.

Dear Dr. Bob,
I have three children, ages four, seven, and eleven years. I try to respect them and their preferences and give them plenty of choices. But it has become a lot of work. How many choices should I give my child?
Sincerely,
Confused Mother

Dear Mom,
Today's world is overflowing with choices. Ordering from your local coffee shops, you have a dizzying array of options: lattes with milk, skim, or low fat; foam or not; one shot or two; iced; or a train with a gazillion flavors. The list goes on and on. Just a cup of regular coffee has selections of sugar, artificial sweetener, cream, half & half, skim, or low fat. Whew! Makes me tired just ordering coffee.

We adults have lived several decades and have a database of experiences that makes our choice-making ability superior. We have made many errors and have learned from them. Children have limited years of experience and are just beginning problem-solving skills. That is why parents need to teach making choices by limiting them at first. Multiple choices all at once are overwhelming for small children. Today's children are frequently asked, "What do you want?" with a universe of possibilities. I was in the local ice-cream franchise the other night and in front of me was a dad-daughter mom-son combo. The children were about four and six years old.

Mom asked, "What flavor do you want, son?"
Son was now peering into the fifteen-foot long case filled with over twenty colorful, tempting flavors.
After a long pause, the son said, "I think the green one. No, the orange one."
Mom responded, "Make up your mind; we are keeping people waiting. Which one?"
Son replied, "I don't know."
Mom finally ordered, "We'll have the orange one," a comment that produced a mini-whining fit until the order was changed to the green one.

Mom then asked, "Which cone?"
Son: "What?"
Mom: "Plain, sugar, or waffle cone."
Son: "You pick."
Mom: "Just decide."

A similar scenario was occurring with dad, who was herding daughter through the same decision-making marathon.

Dad: "Which flavor?"
Daughter decisively picked the pink one. The cone selection was laborious, with the sugar cone winning. Then mom and dad wrestled with "one scoop or two?" Each child wanted two scoops, to which both parents exasperatedly replied, "You never finish one!" The parents overruled their children's decisions and ordered one. I will spare you the toppings exercise of choice. At the end of the treat time, both parents were frazzled and wishing they had not come for ice cream, and the line of parents and kids waiting to choose was out the door.

We all have witnessed children's choice process in restaurants, discount stores, and groceries. Why has this mega-choice movement taken hold? It seems that the principle was to empower the child and encourage self-determination, or probably just to make the child happy. Good intentions aside, the current mega-choice concept has resulted in short-term indecision, frustration, confusion, and an overwhelmed and often melting-down child. Recently during a question-and-answer portion of a seminar, a parent asked, "How many choices should I give my four-year-old?" The parent was about thirty-five years old and my response was, "You have thirty-five years of experience, are able to conceptualize, rationalize, and problem-solve.

Your child has forty-eight months of experience in life, cannot conceptualize, and has only rudimentary problem-solving skills. How many choices do you think you should give him?" She replied, "Obviously less than I am giving." This was not meant to embarrass her, but to make a point we often forget: Our children look to us to help them learn how to make decisions. Giving so many choices without experience and practice is not fair to the child and causes many other problems. This mega-choice process also breeds the notion of entitlement. The child's point of view is, "If my parents always ask me to choose whatever I want, then I must have the right to do it all the time." If a total choice isn't given, anger often results because, in the child's experience, "It's my right!" Societal "experts" have created a monster with ramifications far beyond cone selection. How do parents get off this merry-go-round of pop psychology?

Generations ago, most children under four had their choices made by their parents. By age five-to-six years, the child was given a choice of this or that; by seven or eight, a broader choice was allowed. This mirrors a natural timetable of brain development and problem-solving abilities and their experience of measured choices.

Parents need to provide parameters for children to make choices. Don't give a child a choice you aren't willing to accept. Asking a three-year-old what he wants for lunch can produce a request for ice cream and pickles. What do you do then? Most parents are not ready for that type of answer. Given that circumstance, the parent first tries coaching the child to change her/his mind, and when it doesn't change, a disagreement ensues, unnecessarily disrupting everything.

At age four, my granddaughter was being helped to select a birthday gift for a friend by her mother and older brother. She was asked repeatedly by one, then the other, "What about this as a present, or what about this one?" Finally, she put up her hands and said, "That's just way too many choices!"

Children need to learn to make choices, starting at an early age with one choice: "Do you want this?" The number from which to pick can be increased as they master the skill of choosing. To a two-year-old, a choice of even two things can be overwhelming and oppressive. For many of us, more than a few selections weigh down our decision-making powers; the Starbucks dilemma of one shot or two, skim or regular milk, flavor or not, etc.

Decision-making is powerful and leads to a sense of responsibility, but children need practice learning how to choose responsibly. After the child is seven or eight, the problem is not the choices given, but the responsibility taken for the choices. That's another topic.

CONSISTENCY

Improving the Effectiveness of Discipline. Raising Your Child Without Raising Your Voice.

Repeating over and over, raising your voice, threatening, losing your temper, excessive explaining, constant negotiating, and arguing about every request is not effective parenting and is counterproductive. Once you have established this pattern your child's behavior worsens. How do you break the cycle and become a less hassled screaming, blue in the face parent?

Our goal is to replace the current discipline with benign, firm, "mean it" methods based on an understanding of behavior, temperament, and our expectations. The results will be less punishment and a happier family atmosphere. The suggestions below come from many experts in the field, who *all concur* on the basic methods.

ALTERED ATTITUDES

What follows is a composite of new approaches.

First is to replace *feeling* with *thinking*. Angry feelings transmitted to your child may manipulate him/her to react in the requested manner, but it is likely to be from fear. To reach an objective attitude, first you should suspend your feeling and exam why you are angry. Is it because they made a mistake? Children are supposed to mess up. They are learning. As we have learned with at-risk temperament traits, they really cannot help it. Erase all the thoughts that generate these upset feelings, such as, "They are out to get me," or, "They just want their way," or, "They are being disrespectful," etc. Don't take it personally. Separate yourself, step back, and shift into neutral.

Focus only on the *behavior*, not on your child's mood, motive or that s/he is tired, only the behavior, not the excuse.

Think, respond calmly; don't react emotionally. The *first* question to ask yourself in this objective state is, "Is it temperament? What is setting him/her off?" At first, you will be responding to a behavior or tantrum as it is happening. As you become proficient in being attuned to your child's temperament, you will anticipate and head off the behavior by either altering the expectation, altering the situation to improve the fit, or avoiding the situation until your child has learned to better handle the problem.

The *second* question you ask is, "Is this an important situation I need to respond to now, or can I/should I ignore it?" You *do not* have to respond to every misbehavior! Pick your times. It is more important to respond effectively and consistently than to react in every instance. It is better to ignore than to respond inconsistently. At first, you will need to get used to the objective, non-emotional method, and learn that fewer responses are judicious. The frequently repeated misbehaviors require action before the infrequent ones. Both parents should agree on the top-five list of misbehaviors and first focus on them. When the first five come under control, you may shift the focus to new ones. Focus prioritizing saves parents energy.

Methods of discipline. (See consequences below and in the Appendix.)

Both parents should agree and pre-select consequences that they are comfortable administering. Consequences should be brief, easy for the child to understand, and something that impacts the child's daily life for a short period.

For those under six, most effective is the Time-out, or as I call it, Rebooting. When your computer locks up, you reboot. When your child locks up, you Reboot. (See the Appendix for specifics; you just *think* you understand Reboot/Time-out.) The removal of a favorite possession or activity for short periods of time is more effective than extended time periods such as days or weeks, and the advantage of a five-minute penalty is that you can repeat it often the same day.

Consistency and frequency are much more effective in delivering the message that you mean what you say than long periods of punishment after you have put up with unwanted behavior far past sanity.

Be Brief.

Always be brief and leave no room for argument. "You've done this, it is not allowed, and the consequence is..." **Never over-explain.** Children need to adjust their behaviors; they do not need to understand why! That will come naturally when they have sufficient reasoning powers and an experience base that makes the reason for your action clear. For older kids explanations after the consequence has been completed is fine if brief. Beware the child master negotiator who relishes a discussion to change your mind. Remember all rule changes go through a parent council meeting for the review of the child's proposal, made in writing.

Be Firm

Practice a calm, non-emotional but firm voice. Sound as if there is no plea bargain, no wiggle room, and no chance of changing your mind. "No, do not do that. I expect you to color only in your coloring book, nowhere else. If you do, this (specific consequence) will happen."

Do Not Argue, Negotiate, or Over-explain.

Arguing, negotiation, and over-explaining undermine and short-circuit the learning process. They delay and weaken the necessary urgent message that the behavior is not to be tolerated. It gives your child a chance to change the outcome and weakens the lesson that s/he has made a poor choice. It sends the message to the child that if s/he continues to talk, the rule will be changed, and s/he will *not* suffer the consequences. Arguing, negotiating, explaining is *NOT* a consequence. Children usually only learn if a consequence follows their poor choice.

Limit Warnings

If the activity is dangerous (a Law): "No, that is dangerous. Stop," is sufficient. If the child continues the activity, a consequence swiftly follows. If it concerns a Rule (personal rights and property rights): "You are about to break a rule, respect others' rights/property," is enough. In addressing the daily repetitive things such as manners and "stay out of that," or "please do this or that," a second reminder is okay for children under four years old.

After age four, once is enough! Multiple warnings are ineffective and send the message that you don't really mean what you say.

Be Practical

Children learn best when the consequence quickly follows their misbehavior. At home, it is easier to follow through than it is in the mall, restaurant, church, or grocery store. Creativity and flexibility are needed. Consequences vary with the age; two-, four-, seven, and twelve-year-olds requiring different approaches. Outside the home, misdeeds need to be handled at the time, not later when children have forgotten the circumstances and the consequences will be less meaningful. You may have to remove them from the store, mall, or restaurant to calm them and receive their consequence. After seven or eight years, kids can have consequences delayed until you get home.

Be Composed and Calm

Remove the emotion from your response. I know I have said this many times, but when you are angry, you cannot think well, and it scares your children. They quit doing whatever it is because of your anger, not because of the lesson you want them to learn. Dispassionate correction and enforcement of consequences is your goal in parenting. The outcome of teaching (discipline) is to have your children learn that their choices have consequences. If it is done without emotion, your child will not be afraid to make mistakes, and that is a valuable asset. Regardless of the attitude your child displays after you impose the penalty, *do not waver or engage.* Children often try to save face by saying hurtful things, i.e., "I don't love you," or, "You don't love me," or, "That's not fair," etc. Ignore their replies; your discipline will still be effective.

Make Your Instructions to Children Very Clear

Sometimes we assume that our children understand what we want them to do. Then when they fail to carry out our instructions, we get upset. Make certain that you are very specific in your instructions. "Be good" is a common appeal to children, but what does it really mean? This phrase and many others cause confusion and incomplete compliance with our wishes. The following suggested steps may help you to define more clearly what you expect your child to do:

First, you must obtain your child's attention.

- Move close to your child.
- Say her/his name. (Louder the second time)
- Establish eye contact. (This may require you to say, "Look in my eyes!")

Second, state your instruction clearly

- Give one instruction at a time.
- Give the command, ***"I expect you***..." Give a timeframe for completion. "I expect you to get your shirt changed in the next five minutes." Set the timer.
- The instructions may be in a sequence that is *age appropriate* (under two years, one task; three to four years, two things; four to five, three things. (First, "Go to your room;" second, "Find your blue shirt"; third, "Bring it to me.") After this has been done, the next three can be issued. ("Now take off your yellow shirt;" second, "Put on your blue shirt, and then go put your yellow shirt in the dirty clothes basket.") Realize that distractible children may "forget" during a string of commands. If you repeatedly find your child playing in his/her room, only half completed with the instructions, be patient and break it down to fewer steps in between instruction.
- Use simple words that you know they understand.
- Use any gesture that will enhance the instructions. (Pointing to their room, etc.)
- You may give explanations as to why you want your wishes completed to older children, over six or seven years, but younger children displace the request with the reason and forget the steps. ("You need to change your shirt because you have peanut butter on it, and we are about to go visit Nana.")
- Have them repeat the steps before they start the process.

Examples of *unclear* commands:

- Instructions in the form of a question, such as, "Would you like to put your shoes on?" This implies it is optional when it is not. Be clear that you expect him/her to do it.

- Instructions that begin with "Let's." This implies that you are going to help. State who is responsible for the task. "I expect *you* to..."
- Over-explanation of the "Why" of a request often confuses, sidetracks, distracts, and delays the accomplishment of your request. Brief explanations at the *first* of the request for older children are less likely to lead to forgetting the next words that are the command.
- When you know you have communicated clearly and age-appropriately, then your expectations will be completed more frequently and without confusion.

CONSEQUENCES

All actions, all choices have natural consequences. This is a primary lesson and fact of life.

Unfortunately in our present society many parents are attempting to remove or alter this vital lesson. Current research combined with my forty years of observation during my practice helping families has taught me that this is a mistake. Today's teens and twenty somethings out of their parents' force field of protection are struggling to learn this lesson late, and they are suffering. This lesson needed to be learned in the early childhood years when the consequences were minimal.

Raising a NSEC is very different than raising an easy one. Easy children are less likely to make choices leading to corrective action. When action is required the easy child's response is less likely to lead to resistance and conflict. A stern look is all that is often necessary for the easy child. This doesn't usually work for the NSEC, as you can attest. The easy child's response to correction rarely causes frustration, anger or guilt.

The temperament traits of the NSEC cause a much stronger reaction which requires more structure and fewer options.

Parents of easy kids, teachers, and other caregivers may only have an easy child experience and don't have any understanding of the NSEC's parental challenges or different needs of discipline. Don't feel defensive, upset or shamed by others' comments or ignorance of the requirements to raise a NSEC. You know your child best. Corrective actions, teaching moments and consequences are more frequent and necessary. You can ignore others' opinions confidently because now you have the tools to manage your child! This easy corrective response rarely causes frustration, anger or the following guilt for the parents. The NSEC's responses dictated to the child through their temperament traits are much stronger and require a more structured, less option type response.

One of the most asked questions from my parents is, "What should a consequence be?" Before we address the entire process let's define consequence. A consequence is simply what happens next; it is the reaction to the action. Some are good and some not. When you fix yourself an ice cream sundae the consequence is satisfaction. If you're chopping lettuce without paying attention you may cut your finger, not a good consequence. If your child does what is asked in the allotted time that is a good consequence for him, but if your child chooses not to respond as asked, the consequence is not good. Lesson learned. It is not a punishment. Punishment is retribution with the goal of suffering. I do not believe in a child's suffering; that is what we are attempting to resolve. What should the consequences be? *My concept of consequences is to "reboot."* What do you do when your phone, iPad, or computer sends an error message, locks up, shuts down or crashes? You pause, start over, and reboot. There are cold reboots or hard reboots depending on whether there is loss of power. A cold reboot is a pause as in, "Whoa! Take a deep breath and get yourself together." A hard reboot is loss of power such as in Time Out. The child pauses, gets control and reboots, starts over and resolves the error, melts down or crashes.

Consequences should be easy to impose, short in duration, and "not a big deal." The reason is not to punish, but to stop the progression of the moment that is headed for an unwanted outcome. This makes awarding a consequence an easy, fast, first-resort response. A consequence is a pause in the action and allows your child to reflect on what just happened. This interruption gives time to question, "Was that a good decision or a bad one?" This interrupt step teaches you are responsible for your actions and choices. *This is not about fairness; it is about learning.*

One of the cornerstones of childrearing is to prepare children to be responsible for their choices. Some choices are positive, and some are negative. Having choices means making decisions. There is a force in society today that is trying to sidetrack this basic tenet. It is called "making my child happy." Certainly, we all want the best for our children and would like them to be happy, but two-year-olds will not be happy unless they get their way *now*! They are totally self-centered and with little conscience or the means to decide what is best for them. Children under four years old do not have the refined reasoning capabilities or the experience base to understand the reasons for your decisions. Spending excessive time explaining to your children the whys is unnecessary. Making a child happy in the moment is not in the long-term best interest of the child, nor is it the parents' responsibility.

Why has this concept of catering to children crept into childrearing? I think it is **Guilt.** I have found that much of what parents fail to do for their children is because of guilt. Guilt raises its head when we feel sorry for our child; it has been a difficult day for the child or parent, and saying *no* one more time is too stressful. Many parents feel they should spend more time with their children, and guilt seeps in to sidetrack well-established childrearing principals from being accomplished. Guilt paralyses us from acting like responsible parents. To ease that guilt, we try to please the child. Your parenting focus is to try to remove guilt from the formula of childrearing by teaching our children the choice and consequence lessons *now.* These lessons learned now will allow your children to be truly happy *later.*

Reboot/Time-out is a good first consequence and the default consequence from ages two and a half until about five or six years. Consequences after your child is six are more creative and will be discussed below. Rebooting/Time-out occurs whenever your child breaks a *pre-established* rule or doesn't do what you expected him/her to do within the given time frame. **Immediately** after the infraction occurs, you isolate your child in a boring place for a few minutes. This rebooting has the advantage of providing a cooling-off period, allowing both child and parent to calm down and regain control of their emotions. Problems cannot be solved when you or your child is upset. We lose fifty IQ points when we are angry. Few of us can lose that much IQ and still be an effective problem-solver. Reboot/Time-out is the most effective consequence for toddlers and is more successful than explaining, arguing, threatening, begging, shouting, or spanking. Every parent needs to know how to use rebooting most effectively. I know dads and moms who insist that they have tried time-out and it does not work. But when the "how" of time-out is discussed, it is apparent that their time-out structure was flawed. Parents who are more persistent than their child do not fail. After a Saturday of six or eight time-outs, your child will get with the new reboot program. It also makes children feel secure to have definitive boundaries that are stable and not always changing depending on the parents' mood, energy, or guilt. Reboot/Time-out is to be used to reinforce learning that there is a consequence for ignoring a Law, Rule, or SOP. Time-out is not used for temper tantrums. Time-out is not needed until a child is at least fifteen to eighteen months old. Time-out is unnecessary for children younger than fifteen months because they do not understand what is expected of them and usually respond to verbal re-direction. Developmentally they begin to strongly assert their wishes during the fifteen-to-eighteen-month period. The peak ages for using time-out are from two to five years. During these years, children respond to action more than words.

If you have not used time-out before, go over the rebooting concept with your child before you start using it. Tell your child it will replace spanking, yelling, and other forms of discipline you currently use. Review all the reasons you will use Reboot/Time-out: for example, for breaking the Laws, Rules, or SOPs. Then pretend with your child that she has broken one of the rules. Take her through the steps of rebooting so she will understand your directions when you send her to the reboot location in the future. Teach this technique to your child's caregivers. ***Strive for consistency.***

Children over five need other forms of consequences. Many parents lament that their NSE children do not respond to consequences, or say, "Nothing seems to matter to my child." First, you need default consequences. I prefer to use physical consequences such as push-ups, sit-ups, laps around the backyard. These are Group A-consequences and will be your most-used. How do you customize consequences for your unique child? Casually ask your child, "What are your three most favorite things to play with?" Later ask, "What are your three most favorite things to do?" You guessed it: those are the six new consequences. Group B are things and possessions; and Group C are the activities. Consequences are selected from either group. Vary selection of group: Group A then Group B, etc. The order of your child's preference within the group is also very important. Taking the favorite possession away from the non-adaptive child will most commonly shut her down and nothing works after that. Therefore, take the third-most favorite first, then the second, and only if she has repeatedly and over a short time span refused to do what you expect, take the favorite. Group A is your default or first line of consequences. Group B is primarily used for possession offenses, such as when your child takes a toy from another child or misuses her electronic screen. Then a favorite toy or screen is removed. Cancellation of an outing, a sleepover, a party, or a family get-together can be used for egregious offenses. All these consequences are written down and posted with example offenses listed alongside.

Use pictures for the children who cannot read. You can make a poster of photos of your child refusing to do the expected: taking a toy from a sibling, etc. A circle is drawn around the picture and a line marked through it, then place a photo of the child sitting in reboot/time-out next to the first photo. This gives full disclosure to the child and leaves nothing to chance. When a new consequence is added always explain what is going to happen before the first use.

How long should a possession be removed or a consequence last? ***No consequence should last beyond twenty-four hours.*** When the sun comes up on a new day, the clock starts afresh. This allows you to use the same consequence the next day. For older kids and teens, the length of time varies more widely, but as a rule a week is maximal except in severe dangerous situations such as driving when drinking alcohol or smoking pot. The object of administering time-out is to impress upon your children the consequence of making poor choices. Allow all children, regardless of age, the opportunity to reflect on the rule just broken for a few minutes (one minute per year of age).

Emotions and Consequences

If you become angry with your children when they break a rule, you shift a learning opportunity to a manipulative event. Most children are very attuned to your emotional state and do not like it when you become angry. When you are angry, your children may do what you want, but it is to please you and you have caused them to forfeit a learning opportunity. The important goal of parenting is to teach your children lessons they need in order to become successful in life. This takes a backseat to making your child behave. You will not always be present; they need to learn lessons so they can function well without you.

Location of Rebooting for the Under Six?

The place for reboot/time-out is important. The child's bedroom is not the best choice for rebooting. Most kids' rooms today are a cross between a toy and an electronics store. Laundry rooms are somewhat better. Avoid rooms that are dark or scary, such as closets and basements. **Over the years, I have discovered a better place.** ***It is the bathtub. I call it Tub Time.*** **It is isolated from the family and quiet with a boundary, the sides of the tub. It also is cold, hard, and not a comfortable place, all deterrents to a return.** Do not allow your child to take anything with him/her to time-out, such as a toy, pacifier, security blanket, or pet. The child should not be able to see TV or other people from the location. Tub Time is effective, and they rarely turn on the water. If they do, that infraction can be dealt with by not changing their clothes for thirty to sixty minutes. Warn them that this will happen if they turn it on. (Keep the water temperature low in the hot water tank for Tub Time.)

Rebooting/Time-Out Away from Home

Rebooting can be effectively used in any setting. In a supermarket, younger children can be put in the grocery cart and parked in a corner where you can see them. One mother told me she made a pink tee shirt for her two sons that she had printed with *TIME OUT* on the back and front. They hated wearing the pink tee. That seems extreme to me. I don't believe in shaming children. This mom felt she needed something exaggerated to get her kids' attention. In shopping malls, children can take their rebooting time-out sitting on a bench or in a restroom, but it goes without saying that they remain in your sight. Sometimes a child needs to be taken to the car and made to sit on the backseat for the required minutes. If the child is outdoors you can ask him to stand facing a tree. The most effective way to avoid the need for time-out on an outing is preparation. A trip to Target, Walmart, or the grocery will go much more smoothly if the child knows the expectation. When you say, "We are going to Target this afternoon," your child's immediate expectation is candy and toys. Later at the store when you deny their wishes, you invite a meltdown because you violated the expectations. It would be much better to say, "Kids, we are going to Target for dog food and toilet paper. I have no money for candy or toys today, but we will spend five minutes in the toy aisle for you to browse before we go." This sets the expectations for the outing. Try it. Reboot/Time-out is only effective if the child knows that regardless of the location, breaking laws and rules earns the consequence of time-out. Do not wait until you return home because they will most likely have forgotten why they earned a consequence.

Managing the Time for Reboot/Time-Out

Time-out should be short enough to allow your child to reflect on the original situation and learn appropriate responses.

Setting a portable kitchen timer for the required number of minutes is the most effective way to manage the time of rebooting. ***A timer is the boss.*** When it rings or buzzes, the consequence is over, and no parental permission is required to leave. The timer is not set until the child is quiet. Never take a melting-down child to time-out. Allow the meltdown to resolve, then repeat the original expectation process. If the child refuses again, reboot. ***No talking from the parent during time-out is your rule.*** Action is a consequence; talking is not. Children love the "why game." They have learned that "why" commonly elicits a long-winded diatribe from the parent that they can ignore and gain more time without a consequence, and sometimes it leads to a reprieve. Why is the timer so effective? As I have previously stated, using a timer removes you from the equation and gives the responsibility to the child. It also prevents manipulation. Your child cannot un-ding the timer, but they can un-ding you.

The requirement for rebooting completion is that your child does not leave the location (tub, etc.) until the time is complete. If your child leaves reboot/time-out ahead of time, reset the timer. When you first institute rebooting, be patient. It may take two, four, six resets until your child gets the message that the new rules apply and that you are serious and trustworthy. It may be a long weekend when you first start time-out. Some parents do not consider a time-out to be completed unless the child has been quiet for the entire time. From two to three years of age many children find it very difficult to stay quiet. After age three, quiet time is required. You can tell your child, "Rebooting is a quiet time for thinking. If you yell or fuss, the time will start over."

Releasing your child from rebooting time requires that your child must have completed the time. Your child can then leave when the timer rings. No discussions about why they were sent to time-out should be voiced. It's over and they have rebooted and are ready to start over. There will be a next time; repetition is how they learn.

The Child Who Refuses to Reboot

After age three, any child who refuses to reboot within three or four minutes needs a greater consequence imposed. Do this without emotion, saying, "You have refused to go to reboot, so you cannot play with your favorite toy for an hour." Use the consequences for Rules, such as no phone, tablet, TV, video games, toys, outside play, snacks, or visits with friends, etc. After calmly imposing this consequence, walk away. Do not argue, answer why, or listen to pleas of, "I won't do it again, that's not fair, etc." Your children may be testing your resolve and seriousness. Do not confuse them by inconsistently enforcing a consequence only sometimes. If you address the infraction, *you must carry through.* **It is better to ignore a broken rule than call the child on it and fail to enforce a consequence.** This reinforces the child's belief that you cannot be trusted to do as you say. Some at-risk levels of temperament traits may lead to resistive and defiant behaviors. These less-adaptive children need the parent to advise them of their expectations in advance. Allow a transition time of a few minutes for the children to conform, and if they don't comply, reboot. Demands, commands, and surprise requests require a few minutes for these children to respond. Otherwise, they lock-up, meltdown, and have a fit. "My temperament made me do it" is not an acceptable defense for breaking a rule, but don't short-circuit the learning exercise attempting to overpower the less-adaptive children. You will always cause more suffering for you both.

Some parents work exceedingly hard to prevent their children from making mistakes, and when they inevitably do, the parent becomes upset. Why? Parents who are perfectionistic tend to react with a no mistake philosophy. Perfectionism is a form of nonadaptable, inflexible reacting. The one answer, best case scenario limits problem solving. If this happens to apply to either parent, try to work on reaching a "good enough parenting" goal. (See parenting pearls in Appendix.) Don't get upset when they make poor choices; these mistakes teach them how to make good ones. Allow them the free choice and the consequence that follows. That is the very best way to learn. If you insist on children who make no mistakes, you are dooming them to greater consequences later when you are not there to fix it. Allow the mistakes when they are young, and the consequences are not so great. Early in their lives, it is a lesson learned; later it could be a life-altering penalty that limits their future choices.

What if my child won't reboot?

In general, if a child escapes from reboot/time-out, you should quickly take the child back and reset the timer. This approach works for most children. If a child refuses to stay, the parent should take action rather than arguing with or scolding the child. There are rare incidences that a very, very, very NSEC refuses over and over. This has happened in my long practice of helping hundreds of NSEC less than ten times and usually with the child who has never had any consequences. In these rare cases a parent may temporarily need to hold this non-adaptive child in reboot time-out. Insisting your child reboots teaches your child that you mean what you say and that s/he must comply. Use a chair in the laundry room or hall in this instance. Place your child in the reboot/time-out chair and hold him/her by the shoulders **from behind**. Remaining calm may be difficult but this calmness reflects your resolve. After your child has been restrained in the chair for several reboot sessions, she will usually and finally cooperate. This is dependent on your child's temperament and may take weeks. Persevere; this is an imperative lesson your child must learn! Always avoid eye contact and talking while the child is in time-out. Maintain your calmness and gentle touch to prevent any escalation. Remember, extreme NSEC require even more kindness to understand these lessons.

A last resort for young children who continue to resist sitting in a chair is putting them in a reboot room. You may use a gate blocking the door. If the child leaves the room, then the door is shut and locked if necessary. Most children do not like doors closed or locked. They have a choice: stay in the room and the door remains open or come out and it is shut. *Never argue—act!* Most children need their door closed only two or three times to learn that you are serious. This is drastic but a rare necessity. Consequences are necessary for healthy development. You will not scar their psyches, if you are consistent.

STEP THREE:
BECOMING THE HAPPY FAMILY

CHAPTER 8

DR. BOB'S LAWS, RULES, AND SOPS

Capital Crimes, Felonies, and Misdemeanors

LAWS: Safety issues that could hurt you or someone else. (Capital Crimes, the most serious offense)

CONSEQUENCE: The major lesson for putting oneself or another person in harm's way is to learn why it is dangerous! The consequence is to imprint the lesson, not to punish. Do not get mad, no matter how scared the act made you; that could shift the child's focus away from what is important. The consequence for breaking the Law is "imprisonment," called the Think Tank. One minute per year of age until five, then five to ten minutes for all older children. The Think Tank should be located in the best chair in the house to emphasize that it isn't a normal time-out. Contrary to a regular time-out, after the time is served, the parent does ask a question about the child's action. Why was what you did dangerous? If they can't answer, give them repeated time in the Tank and if they still cannot answer, have a teaching moment.

Always be consistent. (Use predetermined consequences: the Think Tank.)

Consequence for breaking the same law within an hour, or refusing to go to the Think Tank, is the loss of the next major opportunity, outing, sports event, sleepover, or special event with a friend.

Protect yourself and others from harm by:

1. Not running in the house
2. Not climbing or jumping on furniture, in the bathtub, or on the bed
3. Not hitting, kicking, pinching, biting, or pushing people or pets
4. Not playing near or in the street
5. Not crossing the street without an adult
6. Not going to a friend's house or anywhere without permission
7. Not throwing things in the house, including food
8. Not throwing things at people or animals
9. Staying with mom and dad during excursions
10. Not opening doors for anyone other than family or friends approved by parents
11. Not talking to strangers without parent's permission
12. Not playing with knives
13. Always wearing seatbelts in all cars
14. Not eating and playing at the same time
15. Anything else deemed unsafe by parents at the time it occurs

16. Not taking any medicines, drugs, beer, wine, or alcohol, or huffing aerosols
17. Older children and adolescents need age-appropriate refinements to these laws

Customize to your family needs and philosophy.

RULES: Personal Rights and Property Rights (Felonies)

Personal Rights:

Personal space rights

- Everyone has an eighteen-inch space around him or her that is private and should not be invaded without permission. (Except for hugs and kisses, when accepted willingly.)
- Everyone has the right to have peace in his or her space with minimal noise and confusion. This also includes parents.
- Everyone has space that is private, such as rooms, drawers, closets, etc., and should not be entered without permission. (Parents can override this for any safety reason.)

Personal time rights

- Everyone has the right to be alone and have time in her/his space with minimal noise and confusion.
- Play rights: All children have the right to play in any means that is safe, considerate of others' rights, and with the permission of parents.

Activity rights

- Children have the right to participate in any organized activity (sports, dance, music, Scouts, lessons, sleepovers, campouts, and others) with parent's approval and support.

Property Rights

- Children have the right to own and care for property, including toys, games, books, clothes, electronics, and equipment.

CONSEQUENCE: Loss of a previously awarded privilege (TV, computer, electronic game, or telephone time) or removal of property (favorite toy, game, book).
The time lost is a portion of the daily time allowed. This can be a fifteen-minute penalty or one-half of their TV time, or loss of an hour on the phone.

Individualize for each child by making a list of the top-three favorite things to do (personal rights) and the three top favorite possessions (property rights). These are then removed in order of importance or reverse order in the nonadaptive child. **NO CONSEQUENCE LASTS LONGER THAN ONE DAY. EACH DAY BRINGS A CLEAN SLATE.**
The consequence for breaking the same rule within an hour, or refusing to pay the consequence, becomes a broken law.

Personal rights

- Respect = Do not physically invade others' personal or private space.
- Respect = Do not invade others' personal space with noise and confusion.
- Respect = Do not interrupt others' private time.
- Respect = Do not disrupt others' play.
- Respect = Meeting responsibilities to others involved in activities (practicing, being on time, participating to the fullest).

Property rights: Failure to care for property automatically qualifies for removal of that property by the parents for a set period or forever, depending on past care of belongings.

- Respect = Do not take things that are not yours. (No stealing)
- Respect = Do not destroy or mess up others' property. (No vandalism)
- Respect = Do not take things away from people.
- Respect = Do not bother or play with others' possessions without permission.
- Respect = Do not bother or play with parent-controlled electronic equipment (TV, VCR, CD player, computers, tablets, printers, etc.)

Standard Operating Procedures SOPs: *Personal Responsibilities, Manners and Social Conventions (Misdemeanors) CONSEQUENCE: Removal of a pleasure or treat, additional one-time chore, imposing of a fine.*

Personal responsibilities

- Dress self.
- Put up clothes in proper place.
- Put dirty clothes and linens in laundry bin.
- Put away toys before changing activities and at the end of every day.
- Wipe, flush toilet, and close lid.
- Wash hands before and after eating.
- Sleep or play quietly in room during rest time.
- Wash face in the morning, in the evening, and after eating.
- Go to bed on time.
- Brush teeth and floss twice a day.

- Come when called.
- Make bed every morning as soon as getting up.

Manners

- Say "please" and "thank you."
- Shake hands when meeting people.
- Look people in the eyes when talking to them.
- Don't pick nose in public.
- Use a napkin at the table.
- Use a tissue to wipe nose.
- Don't play with food.
- Do not yell at people.
- Treat all others as you want to be treated.
- All other things parents want to add.

Chores: Defined as any job that benefits the family. *Returning to a family-centered instead of a child-centered family requires that* ***all members*** *contribute to the well-being of the family. That means sharing the tasks of managing a home. Everyone helps. Explain that being a member of the family has rights and responsibilities. This increases competence and being needed, the last two requirements for self-esteem.*

Guidelines for Chores

1. Start chores at an early age. Eighteen months to two years is perfect.
2. Show your children how to do the chore in detail and have them repeat it a few times to be assured that they understand. Be specific. "Clean your room" is vague; be specific. "Clean your room" means, "Pick up all toys, clothes, books, shoes and put in the proper place."

3. Introduce one chore at a time with the when/then rule. (When the chores are done, then you can have free time.) Responsibilities always come before rights.
4. The first part of the chore is the chore, and the second part of the chore is a definitive time for completion. (Take out the trash is half a chore; take out the trash by 7:00 p.m. is a full chore.) At 7:01, if the trash is still in the basket, the child did not complete that chore and the consequence is given. No excuses or discussions.
5. Increase the number and complexity of chores as the child grows and develops. See chart below. (I often hear how smart your children are by learning to operate complex electronics to using complex thinking; don't excuse that child from learning how to turn on a dishwasher or washing machine!)
6. Inconspicuously monitor at first. Never redo your child's task. (The results will improve with practice; if they don't, have another learning session.)
7. Do not remind or nag. Remembering when is part of their task.
8. Do not do the chore for them when they forget or refuse.
9. Provide preset consequences for failure to do the chore. Consequences should be logical extensions of the chore. If the child doesn't put up her/his bike, the bike is impounded for a day. Remind the children the family counts on them to do this chore for the family. Rights have responsibilities and they should balance. When a responsibility (chore) is not completed, they forfeit a privilege.

Age-Appropriate Chores

- Under three: start with the above-listed personal responsibilities.
- Ages three to five years old: can set and clear table, clean spills, empty wastebaskets, bring in mail, clear table, pull weeds, hand-vacuum to pick up solid spills, unload utensils from dishwasher, get their own drinks, and fix a bowl of cereal.
- Ages six to seven: Above, plus sort laundry, sweep floors, set table, make snacks of cold foods, PB &J sandwiches, rake leaves, answer telephone, and take messages.
- Ages eight to nine: Above, plus load dishwasher, put away groceries, vacuum and dust, fold and put away laundry, peel vegetables, cook simple food (toast, microwave), mop floor, mow yard with supervision.
- Ages ten to twelve: Above, plus clean bathrooms, wash windows, wash car, iron clothes, do family laundry, cook simple meals, bake cookies, younger sibling care, have neighborhood jobs (mow yards, pet care, etc.).
- Over twelve years: Above, plus most any task an adult can do. At sixteen and after six months' driving experience, adolescents can run errands, such as picking up cleaning, grocery shopping, etc., and be responsible for family meals once or twice a week. This is a great time to cook together to teach and have some one-on-one time. All kids want more one-on-one time with a parent.

START SMALL, BUT START! YOU AND YOUR CHILDREN MAY BE PLEASANTLY SURPRISED AT YOUR ABILITY TO WORK AND PLAY TOGETHER AS A FAMILY.

CHORES ARE MORE IMPORTANT THAN HOMEWORK. BECOMING COMPETENT IS MUCH MORE IMPORTANT THAN MAKING A GRADE.

BECOMING COMPETENT IS A GOAL OF ADULTHOOD.

CHAPTER 9

RESISTING TODAY'S CULTURAL AND SOCIETAL PRESSURES

Are seven after-school activities per child too many, or how to overuse and abuse the SUV, your patience, and memory? "Is this dance, soccer, or tutoring day?"

The Family Versus the Children's Activities

Are you on a merry-go-round of children's activities? Are you constantly questioning that you have too much to do? Have you forgotten one of your child's activities or, worse, left them way past the pick-up time? I hear these concerns almost daily. "Have we overscheduled our children?"

Here are a few more questions to ponder related to your current state and to help you evaluate how your family spends its time:
Do you fall into bed each night drained of energy?

Do you worry about providing all the necessary and best opportunities for your children?

Is it really necessary for your children to have planned activities three to five times a week? What about the families with two or three children? Three activities a week times three kids, and you are struggling to deliver and pick up at nine functions and be present to root for the team.

What are the lessons being learned and are they lasting experiences?

Is the stress of afternoon carpools and "who is going to this practice and who is going to the other child's game" a weekly routine?

When was the last time your family sat and ate five meals together in a week?

Is eating fast food on the run, having meals with only part of the family, or sitting down to dinner after 8:00 p.m. beneficial?

Are your children's activities only for them, or would you or your spouse miss them if they quit? What would you brag about?

Whose idea was the current activities: yours or your child's?

When was the last time you and your spouse sat quietly and just talked?

Is your marriage less of a priority than your child's activities?

When was the last time you just "hung out" with your children?

Do you regularly have one-on-one time with each of your children? Is that less of a priority than your child's practices, games, and tutoring?

Are you feeling guilty? Why are you feeling guilty? Are you not doing something you feel you should or doing something you shouldn't?

Have you contemplated what your family's real priorities are, or do your child's wants prevail?
Will playing sports at seven, nine, eleven years of age teach lessons you cannot?
More importantly: "Are there lessons of life your children are not learning because they are at practice?"
Life is certainly a tradeoff of priorities in today's word. Will the tradeoffs you are making optimally prepare your children for the world they will face?

Today's families spend 22 hours/week less together than twenty years ago: from age two years to age eighteen is 24 months!

Maybe it is time for a meeting of the parental minds to assess your family's priorities.

While I am preaching, let's add another area of today's concerns to your worry box: **electronic connectivity.** If your child is spending more time staring at a screen than playing with others, he is not alone. Our children under eight spend at least two hours a day with some sort of screen (TV, tablet, smart phone, or video game), according to Common Sense Media's 2013 study, *Zero to Eight: Children's Media Use in America*. Children ages eight to eighteen spend, on average, close to forty-five hours per week watching TV, playing video games, instant messaging, and listening to music online. This is a greater amount of time than they spend with their parents or in the classroom, per a study by the Kaiser Family Foundation. While media exposure can be beneficial, research abounds on how much and what subject matter is appropriate for children. Experts say kids aren't getting enough exercise, nor eating a healthy diet, and spending too much time with screens. This is leading to an epidemic of pale, obese children and teens. Another study by the Center on Media and Child Health found that children who watched violent content spent less time with friends than children who watched nonviolent content, resulting in more isolation. Other research has linked television watching to an increased rate of aggressive physical and verbal behavior in children and has led to children with less empathy. Children who spend too much time in front of the TV or computer have "little time for exercising their predispositions for fantasy, imagination, and creativity," writes child development professor and bestselling author David Elkind in his book, *The Power of Play: How Spontaneous, Imaginative Activities Lead to Happier and Healthier Children.*

Here are some pearls to consider for your family and electronics:

- Be certain your kids know your values.
- Be conscious of age-appropriateness; what's okay for eight years isn't okay for the four-year-old sibling.
- Set family rules and stick to them. You know my motto: "If it isn't written, it isn't real." Make it real. Limit screen time, writing exactly the hours allowed for screens per day and post it with the Rules.
- Use technology to control the media. Pre-taped TV programs, DVDs, and videotapes of programs are the best way to control screens. Parents can hit the pause button, talk to their kids, and discuss certain scenes or behaviors when appropriate.

- No screens in kids' bedrooms. Keep screens in a common area where you can keep an eye on things, and all screens are put away at a specific time after dinner to charge for the next day. If they are sneaked out, lock them up at night.

- Mounting evidence is illuminating the effects of watching blue screens within sixty to ninety minutes of bedtime. These wavelengths interfere with sleep. Children need adequate hours of uninterrupted sleep. Teens with phones under their pillows awake to the text tone and that makes for sleepy, irritable youths the next day. Here are some references: https://sleepfoundation.org/ask-the-expert/electronics-the-bedroom

- http://www.digitaltrends.com/mobile/does-blue-light-ruin-sleep-we-ask-an-expert/

- http://www.cnn.com/2016/10/31/health/kids-sleep-screens-tech/

- Use the experts as a resource. *Common Sense Media* is a well-respected source.

CHAPTER 10

PARENTING, OVER-PARENTING, AND JUST-RIGHT PARENTING

Prior to the 1980's being a parent was all about your responsibilities. Keep your children safe, love without expectations or conditions, teach them to solve problems. The final step is for parents to transfer the decision controls as they mature. During this time raising children was the daily process of steering your child through the trials of growth.

Many positive changes have occurred over the past forty years while I have helped parents. One of the most notable is that dads are more involved and engaged in their children's lives. Some things have changed in a negative direction. Along with many other professionals, I am very concerned that we are in the middle of a parental epidemic. This seemingly contagious and widespread outbreak was born of the best intention: to provide the very best for your children, but the unintended consequence has been over-parenting.

How did we get from being a parent, to parenting, to over-parenting?

By the 1990's when sixty percent of women entered the workforce, they were tired at the end of the day and it was very difficult to do the parenting jobs they had done before. That's not the primary reason. I think the main reason was not because they went to work outside the home but because as their parental responsibilities begin to slide, parents, and particularly mothers, began to feel guilty. *Guilt was the change agent that lead us to the current over-parenting.* Because parents felt guilty, they decided to do even more for their children. Those efforts were not in the realm of expectations, responsibilities, consequences and structure but in giving the child more choices, more activities, more things they wanted. All is done to lessen their guilt and make their children happy. This resulted in the shift from a family centered life to a child centered one.

Over-parenting is an attempt to provide the best opportunities and is nurtured by our striving to *make* the best outcomes for our kids: success on all fronts, social, academic, and eventually business, with the resulting high-dollar happiness of *our* dreams. Many parents are so successful in this pursuit of the best that the results are that as they push their children those efforts focus on academic, athletic and extracurricular pursuits.

Their teens are working hard and may be making good grades but are super stressed, reflected by the increasing prescriptions for anti-anxiety/depressants and increased drinking and pot use. This is a struggling attempt to dull their feelings of being severely overwhelmed. They increasingly feel sad and alone and fear growing up in their world of inflated expectations. They are in a bind because they see how hard their parents are working to provide *everything* necessary for a successful life. They dare not say anything to upset their parents and suffer in silence. This leads not only to short-term disabilities but also long-term ones.

Most of you, many with kids under ten, are now saying, "It cannot possibly be so dire." But some of you are saying, "I've seen it in my friends' older kids." It is a difficult thing for parents of a four-year-old to project their parenting actions ten years into the future. I've been professionally watching parents raise their children for forty years and the trends that have shifted our parenting direction have changed, and our children are struggling. Within the bibliography, there is a list of books written in the past ten years with scientific research to prove these concerns are real and widespread.

How can you be a better parent to reverse these trends that threaten our children's future happiness?

Let's back up a minute and start at the beginning. What exactly do we mean by over-parenting? Over-parenting is a severe form of micromanagement of our kids' lives. It is over-directing, removing all obstacles, preventing failure, over-praising, over-scheduling, and all the while this prevents our children from taking their responsibilities. We make sure they have all the freedoms we label "opportunities," but without their corresponding responsibilities. Many teens today rebel at being micromanaged. Parents seem to have an underlying fear their children will suffer, be unhappy, struggle, or have their spirits squashed. Children need to be challenged, have failures, become disappointed and to have struggles. This prepares them for when challenges arise. Then they have confidence to face more complex problems and to solve them on their own. There is a crisis with our teens and twenty-somethings today; they struggle solving life's normal problems. They have had little practice because mom and dad have intervened and solved, smoothed, and prevented these precious teaching moments from occurring early in life. The consequences of failure at seventeen are considerably more than at five. Parents of college-aged children now commonly receive text messages asking, "What do I do?" One of the authors of the recommended books calls the cellphone, "The longest umbilical cord in history." Colleagues of mine who teach undergraduates routinely get texts and calls from their students' parents within hours of passing out grades asking, "Why did you give my child a D?" or similar inappropriate questions. Some of you are saying, "But my child is three, four, or six years old; what does over-parenting look like at this age?" When your four-year-old brings you a problem he or she can't solve, do you solve it? The scores of the Over-parenting quiz reflect the degree of over-parenting.

Family structure has deteriorated over the past twenty years. Parents have removed or greatly lessened their children's expectations and responsibilities. This old mainstay of raising children has been replaced with, "Oh, let them enjoy themselves; they will grow up soon enough." There are no laws, rules, or standard operating procedures guiding family boundaries. I have parents who routinely state that their mornings are "hell." Trying to get the kids up, dressed, and ready to leave for school leaves both parents with heartburn and exhaustion before 7:30 a.m. each day. Why? These parents wake their children, reawake them, nag them to hurry and get dressed, or help the five- and six-year-old to do so. The parents are constantly prying the kids away from the TV and urging them to hurry up, get their backpacks, and get to the car. Often, all are late. Commonly, the parents are squabbling in the background with each other to *please help me with this!* Sound familiar? The answer is simple. Start with a schedule and an alarm clock for each child over age five. Have a time written beside each necessary step on their schedule: 6:45, alarm; 6:50, complete going to the bathroom, etc. They are dressed and ready to walk out the door at 7:30. No breakfast until they are ready to leave and no TV until breakfast is complete. Sounds anal-retentive but it is better than parents' developing an ulcer by age thirty-five. Schedules do work. Older kids can help younger ones. Yes, what used to be typical has vanished, and I don't know why. One of my parents returned after this discussion of stressed mornings to say to me, "My mornings are a delight. I have exercised and am drinking my coffee when my three children come down to breakfast." She thought at first this was a crazy idea but found it an easy goal to attain and her kids were proud of themselves.

The family meal was a routine in most families, but now occurs in only 40% of homes three nights a week. Most families eat out over 40% of meals. Eating in the car and on the run has become the norm. Research has shown us that family meals are important for the adult preparatory lessons learned during these sharing times. If mom and dad are running in different directions, shuffling children from one activity to another, the opportunity for sit-down meals together is lost.

I have a hard time believing that group activities and team sports are teaching children more than their parents could.

Over-praising is another form of over-parenting that has adverse long-term consequences. Many are saying, "How can telling my five-year-old he is special going to hurt him?" It leads to entitlement and disappointment when as a teen the outside world doesn't find him special. He is special to you, but tell him you love him, not that he is so great.

The model for praising is to praise the effort, not the outcome. "You should be proud you worked so hard on your homework," not, "I'm so proud of you: you got all the answers right; you are so smart!" Po Bronson, in his book, *Nurture Shock*, has a chapter, "The Inverse Power of Praise." He discusses research findings that show by praising outcomes such as grades, touchdowns, and awards, many children become overwhelmed with the pressure to continue to perform at such a high level. As they grow and it becomes harder, they simply give up and take the easy way to avoid failure and their parents' disapproval. Be careful with the fad of saying "good job," particularly when the job they did isn't really that extraordinary an accomplishment. Solving their problem for themselves is all the reward children need to build real confidence. If you help too much, they must give you credit.

The best model parents can reflect to their children is a base of reality and problem-solving skills, not an encyclopedia of directions. They don't have to remember what you said; they can solve it themselves and their confidence grows.

Do you impose activities on your children or are their activities of their own choosing? **Overscheduling** is overwhelming to many kids. If your answer is, "But it will be good for them," you are over-parenting. I have families with two kids that need the help of Microsoft Outlook to manage their seven- and nine-year-old children's after-school activities, to determine who transports who, what time will everyone eat and what and where. ***If you ask most children and teens, as surprising as that seems, what they would like most from their parents, they overwhelmingly respond, "More time with my parents."*** Not another activity with mom and dad rooting from the sideline. As I have stated before, today's parents spend twenty-two hours less a week with their children than parents did twenty years ago, equaling forty-eight days a year less and 2.3 years lost by age eighteen when the children leave home. Extracurricular activities for children under ten years of age are overrated and produce fewer positive effects than free time hanging out with parents or friends. This is not applicable if your child considers an electronic device a friend.

Lack of consequences is another vanishing act in the over-parenting scheme. Not punishment, but consequences. You have read my absolute belief in this so I will not belabor that point.

Under-parenting is not doing too little; it is when parents don't do what should be done such as saying no and defining what is expected. Wow, you can over-parent and under-parent at the same time. In other words, making their children's lives too easy. That handicaps children, limits long-term growth, and prevents their problem-solving and ultimate success. Under-parenting results when parents fear that their child does not possess the toughness to withstand a disappointment. Parents do not believe in their child's abilities. Instead of helping their child develop the tools to withstand disappointments, they intervene and fix it, try to lessen the hurt. Say your five-year-old isn't invited to a friend's birthday party, so you call the friend's mom and say they must have forgotten to ask your child or petition all the moms in the class to always invite all the kids in a class. Disappointments happen and will increase in the hurt potential if the parent doesn't have faith that the child can understand and withstand disappointments. Today is witness to the fact that many teachers are being asked to revise their child's grade, coaches are petitioned to play their child more, and generally parents interfere with the natural way things happen and do not prepare their children for these setbacks. This results in less resilience for their kids and long-term unhappiness. Under-parenting is not helping prepare their children for the world they will face. If they don't learn it when the stakes are low, how will they withstand the disappointments, failures, and unfairness of the world when the stakes are high? True under-parenting is not raising their children to develop skills for the future.

You are all great parents trying to do the best for your children but caught up in a societal movement that has proven to cause our children to struggle.

Just-right parenting is of course the reverse of over-parenting and under-parenting. Above all, it is teaching your children to solve problems, be self-reliant, and take their responsibilities. This may sound like you are pushing your child into adulthood way too early, but if done as the child develops, and if at each step responsibility is increased, and you are patient with their failures as they learn, they will be successful. These parents have a strong belief their children will take the punches life throws by developing the tools they need. This will ensure their children will find their own brand of success. Parenting is a challenge, but when the groundwork is laid early, it is manageable, and your children will truly thank you for preparing them for their future lives. Raising children has no shortcuts. This constant process is like the adage, "Life is like licking honey off a thorn." The joys of those moments of clarity outweigh the "What do I do now?" moments of confusion and doubt. Relish the ride, struggles, successes, suffering and joys; they will define you and your child and become the memories of your life.

CONCLUSION

WHAT DOES SUCCESS LOOK LIKE?

Can your children be anything they want or dream to be?

Contrary to what most children hear from their parents and teachers today, they may *not* be capable of becoming what they dream. Many children are wooed to believe this rather wonderful idealistic thought, but realistically life is more complicated than a belief and a dream. False hopes delay the genuine search for a direction in life. Many parents who have a child with athletic ability begin planning a professional sports career by the time the child turns six. The likelihood of a professional sports career is comparable to winning a jackpot at the local casino. Only the *very* exceptional athlete becomes the pro, not the very good one, but the best in the area.

Dr. Jean M. Twenge, a college professor and author of *Generation Me: Why Today's Young Americans Are More Confident, Assertive, Entitled—and More Miserable Than Ever Before*, rails against promoting this concept of "You can be anything you want to be." She sees daily examples of students who are unhappy, disillusioned, and depressed because what they dreamed, or what their parents dreamed for them, and what is possible for them is a mismatch.

Dr. Mel Levine, in his book, *Ready or Not, Here Life Comes,* repeatedly states that children and twenty-somethings are ill-prepared to face the real world by carrying the myth of, "Be your dreams." Both authors share their concerns that these disillusioned, discouraged, and depressed youths and young adults are battling the real world with insufficient tools, and a lack of realism and understanding of who they really are.

How Do You prepare children for the future?

Parents begin to think of the answer to this question earlier than any past generation. In my office I hear concerns about children as young as three or four. There is more stress over the best preschool, school, grades, and the best sport, the best college, the best way to prepare our children to succeed in the real world. Parents who don't hop on this current roller-coaster ride to their child's future are made to feel guilty and are regarded by many as poor parents.

I see children in my practice who have a fixation on the wrong things they think will prepare them for their coming adult lives. Their GPAs, SATs, and athletic endeavors have become the mantra of the children and their parents. A school principal friend of mine told me recently a student's father came to see him for advice about the best baseball batting coach for his son who was four years old. Parents enroll their progeny in SAT/ACT prep courses in middle school. They seek the perfect fit for the perfect college and have predetermined grandiose outcomes of their years beyond college. The teen pressures from parents to be admitted to the best college is the current high school obsession. Getting a good education seems less important than where you go. What you do with your life has very little to do with the above focus. A very interesting book about the college selection process is: *Where you go is not who you will be: An Antidote to the College Admissions Mania* by Bruni Frank. I have interviewed hundreds of people for jobs, both professional and nonprofessional positions, and have yet to ask for a GPA or SAT score, or what sport they played or even where they went to college. Neither have any of the executives I know. We are much more likely to ask what occupies their off-time: do they perform volunteer service, or what is their passion. Part of any hiring assessment encompasses how they play with others, are they kind, can they communicate both verbally and in writing. Many families spend more time planning a vacation, camps, and extracurricular activities than endeavoring to discover who their children really are, what their strong points are, and how to foster growth in those areas. College is not for all kids. Their skill sets may be better suited for an associate degree, a trade, retail, food service, etc. Help your children define their niche in this world that fits their personality, skills and proclivities.

How do you best prepare your children for success? What are the best indicators of a successful adulthood?

Pick your three favorites from this list:

1. Involved parents
2. Good social skills
3. Athletic prowess
4. Happy childhood
5. The best schools
6. Strong moral principles and church attendance
7. High grades
8. Ability to delay gratification
9. Willingness to do the unpleasant and difficult task
10. A fit of career and talents

If you picked any of the first seven choices, they have not been proven to determine long-term life success. The last three have been shown over and over, in study after study, to determine what predicts success. Prediction comes from a child's qualities, not experiences. The four- or five-year-old willing to wait five minutes for four M&Ms rather than having two immediately, becomes the successful adult. The children who persevere in the face of whatever obstacle appears will become a success according to their talents. The children whose skill sets, and talents match career demands are happier, more content, and successful.

Am I saying that grades don't matter? They only matter as it relates to the last three choices listed above. Do good schools, involved parents, and a happy childhood matter? Certainly, they matter, but they are not predictors of long-term future success. Many parents today encourage the reverse of delaying gratification by granting their children's wishes as fast as possible. A recent study revealed that two-thirds of parents would give their child whatever they wanted if they could afford it, and immediately. Few parents today insist on their child having chores. This is one of the best ways to encourage a child to do what they do not want to do. Doing for your children what they can do for themselves prevents learning to do the unpleasant and difficult. During my seminars, I frequently ask the parents to raise their hands if they have done three or four things today that they didn't wish to do. Most all raise their hands. Then I ask the parents to raise their hands if they have had asked their children to do two or three things the child didn't want to do any time in the past week. There is always a significant pause and less than half raise their hands.

The preparation journey begins during the child's first ten years, with the exploration of interests, talents, proficiencies, and matching temperaments. Spend time discovering your children's talents and passions and ask them questions to ponder and give them problems to solve and chores to do. These are the things that prepare your child for the future.

Realize your children may not be able to be anything they dream of being. Being a celebrity rock star may be out of the question.

There will be areas that do not fit your child's skill sets, talents and temperament. I have counseled teens who plan a career in sales and marketing who are shy and have minimal social skills. Can a shy person become a good salesperson? Certainly, but why concentrate on changing what is natural (being cautious) rather than emphasizing that trait in a field that rewards caution? One of my patients had a child who was very slow to adapt but planning a career in air-traffic control because he loved airplanes! Obviously, that is a mismatched career choice. Parents in these situations have remarked that they knew their child's chosen path would be a challenge, but they did not want to squelch him/her. Better now than after a few years of the disappointments of unrealistic dreams.

The next step is to help your children eliminate the areas that do not fit their talents. Then focus on the child's positive strengths.

Ask yourself some questions about your children. Are they right-brained: creative, empathetic, sensitive, conceptual, expressive, intuitive, and feeling or left-brained: analytical, detailed-oriented, logical, organized, and reserved? What are their favorite things to do? Do they like to put things together, solve problems, express ideas, draw, sing, help people, socialize, or plan things? How do they spend their time; what turns them on or off? Do they like change or hate it? Are they comfortable with rules or do they chafe against them?

These exercises help you as parents begin to go beyond the surface intuitive knowledge you have gained about your children to explain who they are and discover who they are not. This helps you to encourage your child to try activities that nurture ingrained talents. If you have a very kind, empathetic child, you may want to encourage her to volunteer as a candy striper or to read to the elderly in a nursing home.

This is not to say that a shy child should not be encouraged to strengthen a weak skill and practice speaking up in class.

There are several tests available to help children narrow fields of interests. Don't prematurely attempt to select a profession. Selecting a profession within a field of interest is your child's personal discovery journey. That trip is aided by taking exploratory courses in the field and talking to and observing people in that field. It is a journey for them and without you inserting your dreams upon them.

Many children go to college with a parental predetermined major only to change it several times.

What are the qualities of a successful teen/young adult?

Parents worry are they doing enough to prepare their children for the reality living as an adult. What are the qualities that mark a mature twenty something?

Throughout the teen years what you are looking for is progress. It is not mistake free living but always learning from mistakes and moving on. What follows are the areas to focus your support. Praise their efforts: "I know you had some tough choices and decisions, but you should be proud of the way you handled them."

The first signs of maturity are when a child begins to take the **initiative**. This first step has an opportunity to begin when you stop reminding your child and expecting that they remember. Let the natural consequence follow, or in the case of chores, add another one when one is forgotten.

A close second is when you see your children understand the task must be done, and, without complaining, persist until it is done. This builds a work ethic and commitment to what needs to be done over what they want to do. It proves their self-worth and esteem.

These signs of self-management and reliance are the blast off points to maturity.

Strong **Executive function skills** are needed to accomplish these milestones. Initiating a project first requires focus, attention, planning, organization and time management. These are skills you have helped them to strengthen or develop in their first ten years. The last of the executive function skills to master is self-monitoring. Parents, your goal is to help your children make you unnecessary as a reminder of tasks to be done.

Seeking success outside the home by working is also a critical experience of adulthood. By age sixteen having a job allows your child the experience of a boss, taxes and customers. Each of these certainly opened my children and grandchildren's eyes to the real world and gave a glimpse of reality to come. It also made them appreciate their parents!

Mastering **academic skills** is more important than the actual grades. Not all children are academically inclined and may not be on a college track, but do need to appreciate the value of learning, the discipline of study habits and the curiosity learning creates.

Maturity also comprises health maintenance, limitation of risks, substance use, media overuse and managing a decent diet and sleep routines.

Developing healthy connections with same and opposite sex, treating others with empathy and coping with conflict are vital skills.

Temperament traits, as you now know, play a huge role in how easy or difficult accomplishing these goals is for any child and you will play a definitive role in helping.

INTRODUCTION

My goal is to help parents and children struggling with behavioral and learning issues by giving professional advice to raise their easy or NSE children. Please know each sheet is only part of the resources available and it is best to have all the information. Read the entire book. You can find additional material from my blog www.drbobsnsec.com to help you.

HELP SHEETS

HELP SHEET #1 Getting to Now What: Preventing Lockups, Tantrums, Meltdowns, and Trips to the Mudhole
HELP SHEET #2 The High-Sensory Threshold Child and Social Relationships
HELP SHEET #3 The Low Sensory Threshold or Highly Sensitive Child
HELP SHEET #4 The Very Negative, Always Complaining, Glass Half-Full Child
HELP SHEET #5 The Low Persistence, Distractible, Short Attention Span Child
HELP SHEET #6 Improving the Effectiveness of Discipline: Raising your child without losing your cool
HELP SHEET #7 Over-Parenting Quiz
HELP SHEET #8 Top Ten Parenting Pearls

TEAR AND SHARE SHEETS

1. NSEC Rating Scale
2. Over-Parenting Quiz
3. Behavioral Cascade
4. Laws, Rules, and SOP's
5. Behaviors and Remedies

Bibliography
Glossary

HELP SHEET #1

Getting to Now What: Preventing Lockups, Tantrums, Meltdowns, and Trips to the Mudhole

THE SECRET OF UNLOCKING A "LOCKUP" IS GETTING TO "NOW WHAT."

A lockup is what happens when a child is faced with a problem he cannot solve. The brain locks up. The child's brain cannot get to the next step in solving the problem: "Now what do I do?" This help sheet is the process to get your child to this step.

Temper tantrums and meltdowns are usually viewed by parents, teachers, grandparents, caregivers, and most everyone as "the way children get their way." When a child exhibits this behavior in public, these same people interpret it as "a child out of control," and all have their way to handle it. Some embrace the attitude, "That child just needs to be shown who is boss." (Using power and punishment if necessary.) There is often a whispered statement, "Today's parents just let their children run wild." They need to give that child some punishment!"

A tantrum is usually viewed as purposeful behavior for children to get their way.

What if a tantrum occurs in response to the child's being overwhelmed and not possessing the necessary skills to solve the dilemma? Children are commonly overwhelmed by expectations of their caregivers or their environment that conflicts with their temperament. In these situations, the child first locks up. This lockup may be slow to occur or can occur in an instant. If some resolution of the issue is not accomplished (solving this problem), the lockup proceeds to a tantrum. These tantrums, meltdowns, or driving into the mudhole can last from a few minutes to several hours.

The length of the tantrum depends on the child's temperament. Less persistent and distractible children tend to have shorter spells of no control in contrast to the persistent and non-distractible child. Developmentally, children under two years old are more easily frustrated, and when faced with a problem, may lock up more frequently than an older child. By three years of age, easy children have developed some control over frustrating situations. "Not-so-easy" children may become overwhelmed and drive into the mudhole because of temperament traits in the at-risk range, no matter how old they are.

The secret to the management of a tantrum is to recognize the warning signs and to intervene before the meltdown occurs. Once a tantrum is underway, there is no stopping it. The child has driven or been pushed into the mudhole. His/her tires spin, mud flies everywhere, and s/he stops only after running out of gas. Children can cause the mudhole experience themselves or a caregiver can be the cause. An example of driving into the mudhole is when a non-adaptable child comes to breakfast having decided earlier that, "I'm having Frosted Flakes for breakfast." The desire is ingrained, and when he opens the box, there are no Frosted Flakes. He may drive directly into the mudhole because he does not possess the problem-solving skills to alter his predetermined choice. Another example of pushing a child into the mudhole is a parent demanding that a non-adaptable child, who is busy with her own project, "Stop that now and go to the car. I said do it now, right NOW!" The non-adaptable child is unable to proceed; she doesn't possess the skills to shift from where she was to where you want her to go in less than a minute. Your expectation is a poor fit with her temperament and produces a conflict she is incapable of solving.

The secret to managing tantrums, meltdowns, and trips to the mudhole is to:

- Appreciate how your child is wired
- Avoid unrealistic expectations
- Recognize the lock-up state
- Use your Key to unlock the locked-up state

What is the Key?

The Key is a technique with four steps to arrest the lock-up behavior:

1. Recognize the lock-up state
2. Teach your child to stay calm

3. Teach your child to think
4. Teach your child to solve the problem

First, recognize that you only have a short time to become aware that your child is locking up. This requires that you become very attentive and/or become a soothsayer. Becoming a soothsayer is easier than it may appear. Many of my parents come in exclaiming that they could head off several mudhole wallowings by predicting their child's reaction to certain situations. Review your child's temperament profile to remind you of the situations that easily overwhelm and derail your child. Those are the expectations that are counter to your child's temperament.

If you expect:

- The very active to sit still for extended periods
- The shy child to greet a strange person
- The less adaptive to "Do it now!"
- The non-persistent or distractible to focus for long periods
- The sensitive to ignore loud, smelly, hot situations

You are asking for a lockup followed by a tantrum.

When your children are first experiencing or are about to experience a lock-up situation, teach them the following routine:

1. Gently raise your hand's palm toward them. This implies for them to Stop.
2. Next, both parent and child take several (at least four) slow deep breaths.
3. When you know you and your child are calm, lower your hand.

4. Parent speaks first to the child.
5. "You are getting locked-up."
6. "What is bothering you?" Then really listen and help the very young explore with words the reason they are becoming upset. Repeat their words.
7. Your next words must be uttered with empathy and understanding and without saying, "No!" No is the mudhole-pushing word.
8. Say instead, "I'm not saying you can't do that, but listen to my concerns."
9. List why you have a problem with their desires.
10. Then rapidly, before they drive toward the mudhole, say, "This is a problem; how are we going to solve it?" If you can keep the conversation on a thinking level and not on an emotional level, your results will be more successful.
11. Next, explore the options, saying, "What are our options?" This is an important exercise in problem-solving. This teaches what is possible.
12. Next, explore the consequences of each option. "If we do that, it could hurt you; we don't want that, do we?"
13. Compromise when possible if nothing dangerous or precedent-setting is at risk.

Obviously, this exercise is not always possible or necessary. When children do not have problem-solving skills, this learning experience will teach them how to manage their deficiencies and prevent embarrassing moments that label them, limit them, and decrease their potential to maximize their talents.

HELP SHEET #2

The High-Sensory Threshold Child and Social Relationships

High Threshold or less-sensitive children have decreased sensitivity to sounds, lights, colors, textures, temperature, pain, tastes, smells, dirt, etc.

They have

- Minor interest in the taste of food
- Under reaction to pain, such as minor cuts and scrapes
- Less appreciation of temperature changes, loud noises, and confusion
- Less empathy for others
- Less awareness of others' space and presence
- Less awareness of nonverbal social cues
- Less awareness of implied social messages

These children need higher levels of sensory input before changes in their behavior are seen. Repetition is needed to learn socially accepted responses. Their pain threshold is high; attention should be paid to any distress from pain. They often need social clues explained and reiterated. They may need failed social relationships and expectations explained in more detail. "I know that it is difficult for you to respect others' space. I know it is hard for you to understand what others are experiencing. I know it does not bother you when someone does that, but it does bother others."

They may seek increased sensory stimulation, such as louder noises, etc., and you may have to speak louder to get their attention. Repetition is needed to learn rules and socially accepted responses, have respect for personal space, and for others' feelings.

If a child also is non-adaptive, social issues may be a significant problem. Social interaction requires rapid processing, complex thinking, and flexibility, with which these children have difficulty. Their process speed is slower, and their thinking more concrete and rigid. The rapid nonstop nature of social interaction is automatic for the adaptable and sensitive who "get the nonverbal cues," but very frustrating for the less adaptable and less sensitive.

It becomes easy to understand that social interaction creates a constant challenge and mystery to these children. They tend to want to "do it their way" because they can't process quickly. They tend to find friends who are adaptable or younger and who will go along with their directions, desires, and plans.

Less-sensitive children often have trouble identifying how they feel. Learning about their feelings is the first step in helping them learn to interact more appropriately.

Here are the steps to teach your child

Identifying the Feeling

- "What is happening to your body when a feeling occurs?" (Stomach aches, heart rate increases, breathing stops or becomes fast, mouth shape changes, face gets hot, etc.) The next time your child registers a feeling, seize the moment to ask questions and explore, "How are you feeling?"
- "What happened just before you had the feeling?" (Events causing the feeling: someone surprised you, scared you, took something away, gave you a toy, etc.)
- Realize that feelings are a natural response.

Labeling the Feeling

- Positive or negative. (Use chart to explore feelings and words to identify.)
- Put a word with a feeling. (Parents can teach many new words to fit the feelings: "Exasperated, frustrated, I'm at my wits' end!")
- Think about what caused the feeling, so they can recognize it when it occurs again. (You told me to, "Do it now, and I was in the middle of something important to me. I got upset, angry, mad, frustrated, exasperated, etc.")

Express the Feeling

- Express the feeling to others. ("When that happens, it makes me feel...")
- Choose the best behaviors to deal with your feelings. (First, take some deep breaths to calm down so you can think, then state the feeling and resultant problem. Explore how to solve the problem in everyone's best interest, if possible.)

Put Yourself in the Other Person's Shoes

- Remember, these children often are not bothered by hurt feelings. Asking them,
- "How would you feel if...?" doesn't work to teach them the lesson.
- Explain how others may feel, "When you do...it makes most people upset, angry, sad, etc. Be careful not to do that so you won't cause..."
- Use any conflict as an opportunity to role-play and teach the more appropriate responses.
- Be empathetic. These children are not intentionally being insensitive; they do not have the natural automatic capacity to interrelate and communicate easily. They must learn. You will have to teach them.

Here are some social skills that all children need to master, but are not easily learned by the less sensitive:

- Listening to others
- Understanding that others' points of view are important
- Conversing
- Convincing others
- Knowing your feelings
- Expressing your feelings kindly
- Recognizing and expressing empathy
- Negotiating
- Conflict resolution

HELP SHEET #3

Very Low Threshold/ Highly Sensitive Child

A highly sensitive child perceives and responds more to his/her five senses of: taste, sight, touch, smell, and sound. This enhanced sensitivity to sounds, lights, colors, textures, temperature, pain, tastes, smells and touch may overwhelm these children and cause them to lock up or shut down. Their clothes have to feel right, which can make dressing a problem; if they don't like the way foods feel in their mouth or taste, these preferences may become an issue. They may seem to overreact to pain such as minor cuts and scrapes; they may feel too warm or too cold when others don't. The very positive accompanying traits are their very empathetic and awareness of others' space and presence, and very attuned to nonverbal social cues and physical changes. They are alert to danger and read the emotional climate quickly. S/he is an intuitive communicator, has superior skill in knowing how s/he is feeling and how others are reacting to what is going on. Knows when others are upset, happy or distressed. These children are very good story tellers and make great and loyal friends. Meeting a kind person in our daily routines always creates a good warm feeling; this is the type person these children become.

Avoid labeling your child as whiny, fussy, picky, particular, hard to please, too soft hearted, a worry wart, etc. Be empathetic to his temperament with statements such as, "I know that really loud noises, odors, etc., bother you. I know this tastes funny, feels tight, is too loud, etc., to you." I know you are worried about your friend, etc." Acknowledge the child's perceptions as valid. Recognize that the child is really bothered by some sensory input and not just being contrary. Do not challenge the child's perception; it is real to him/her. Make these children comfortable. Give them permission to feel as they do. They can be easily overwhelmed by high levels of commotion, uncertainty, sensory overload of smells, noise, bright light, any rock concert type atmosphere.

Appreciate your child for this unique trait as a sensory and emotional bellwether. Although she may be unhappy that her clothes are scratchy, tight, loose, or that the temperature is not just right, she will be a wonderful friend, a kind person and bring much joy all around. Because of this hypersensitivity, realize that when her world is out of whack it must be fixed before she can proceed. This temperament trait is neurologically wired; she is not being difficult. These children suffer for others, and you must try to understand this is a strength. Be patient and use those moments to teach your child to put the circumstance in perspective. Learning to be more resilient is important for self-protection. When s/he becomes overstimulated/overwhelmed, teach the calming techniques we have mentioned. Go through the problem-solving process of Getting to Now What to address all possible alternative solutions. Embrace and celebrate your child's special traits.

HELP SHEET #4

The Very Negative, Always Complaining, Glass Half-Empty Child

This child tends to be negative in mood with reactions more often tending toward distress or discomfort. Parents should not feel responsible for this temperament characteristic nor guilty about the child's apparent distress. This first reaction to most things has absolutely nothing to do with the child's state of happiness. It may seem that way, but it is not a reflection of unhappiness. Parents did not cause this disposition nor can they "fix" it.

This child's first reaction to a request, stimulus, or idea is most often negative. He may appear cranky or serious and is not happy about very many things. He seems to look for problems and uses the glass is always half-empty type responses.

Often children with this trait are described as complainers, whiners, pouters, and gripers, never-satisfied contrarians. Try to avoid these labels and ignore their constant negative mood, while teaching a more positive or silent response to situations. Most do not like to be around this negativity and socially it may prejudice others' feelings toward this child. It may also predetermine their reactions to situations. Softening of this trait is a long-term teaching goal.

You cannot make things positive for this child. Keep your reaction neutral and give the child time to adjust or get on with his activity. Say to yourself, "The negative response is the behavior of my child's temperament. There is nothing wrong with my child, and *I shouldn't confuse this mood with unhappiness.*" Ignore as much of the negative content as possible. Do not try to make this child happy; it will usually make things worse. These children tend to be pessimistic and unrealistically negative in their belief of the positive possibilities in a situation. The positive side of this is that all groups need a naysayer to balance a group's planning. The thought expressed by the negative person is often the reason for a backup plan that saves the day.

HELP SHEET #5

Tips for Children with Low Persistence, Distractibility, Short Attention Span

For Parents of Children Under Ten Years Old:

1. Maintain eye contact with your child when you give directions or instructions and make them clear and concise.
2. Give directions as simply as possible. Break task into single parts and lead the child step by step.
3. Having the child make a video in his mind following the step by step instructions rather than remembering what you said is more productive. These kids are more visual learners and this exercise helps them to remember.
4. Ask your child to repeat directions (pictures in their head) to make certain s/he understands.
5. Repeat in a calm manner when the child hesitates.
6. Redirect attention as often as necessary to keep him/her on track and focused. "Let's get back to the task. That's interesting for later, but let's finish this now."

7. Have specific times for specific tasks to allow the child to plan ahead and be ready to focus his/her energy on the project or specific responsibilities.
8. Develop a daily assignment chart, day timer, or a computer program to delineate tasks and a time in which to do them. Organization of responsibilities will be a lifelong need. Start now.
9. Avoid complex task completion when you know that your child is tired. Fatigue increases frustration and stresses self-control.
10. Plan ahead and teach your child to do the same. The more a child knows what is expected, the better s/he can plan.
11. Remain calm, state your expectations, and offer encouragement: "I know that you can do this. Take your time."
12. Always be aware of your child's energy level and the need to express it regularly. The younger the child is, the shorter the periods of concentration interspersed with activity should be. Praise their efforts: "You must be proud of yourself, you worked hard."

For Children Over Ten Years Old

- **Keep a daily schedule:** Set a schedule and write it down to wake up, eat, bathe, do chores, and go to sleep about the same time each day. Responsibilities always come first, then fun.
- **Cut down on distractions:** When tasks require focus, eliminate everything else, (TV, music, others' activities, etc.)

- **Organize your space:** Find a place to work that offers no distractions. Find a home for all your stuff, always replace it, and it will not get lost.
- **Use checklists, calendars, phone notes:** Written (pen and paper or electronic) reminders for homework, and to-do lists will limit forgetting and help keep the family on track.
- Limiting choices cuts down on children's being overwhelmed. Setting fewer steps and tasks, combined with shorter bursts of attention and focus, increases the success rate. Break down into small goals. Spend time evaluating what should be considered first, second, etc. Set your priorities.

HELP SHEET #6

Improving the Effectiveness of Discipline:

Raising Your Child Without Losing Your Cool

Repeating over and over, raising your voice, threatening, losing your temper, excessive explaining, constant negotiating, and arguing about every request is not effective parenting and is counterproductive. Once this pattern is established, behavior usually worsens. How do you break the cycle and become a less-hassled parent?

Our goal is to replace the current discipline with benign, firm, "mean it" methods based on an understanding of behavior, temperament, and our expectations. The results will be less punishment and a happier family atmosphere. The suggestions below come from many experts in the field and *all concur* on the basic methods.

Altered Attitudes

First is to replace *feeling* with thinking. When angry feelings are transmitted to children, they may manipulate the child to react in the requested manner, but it may be through fear.

To reach an objective attitude, you must first suspend your feeling. Shift into emotional neutral. Children are supposed to mess up. If it is due to temperament, they cannot help it, but they are still responsible for their behavior, even though it is due to their brain wiring. Erase your thoughts that generate upset feelings, such as, "They are out to get me; they just want their way; they are being disrespectful, etc." Do not take it personally. Separate yourself, step back, and shift into neutral.

Focus only on the *behavior*, not on your child's mood or motive.

Think and respond calmly; do not react emotionally.

The **first** question to ask yourself in this objective state is, "Is it temperament? What is setting him/her off?" At first you will be responding to a behavior or tantrum as it is happening. As you become proficient in being attuned to your child's temperament, you will anticipate and head off the behavior by altering the expectation, altering the situation to improve the "fit," or avoiding the situation.

The **second** question you ask is, "Is this an important situation I need to respond to now, or can I/should I ignore it?" You do not have to respond to every misbehavior! It is more important to respond effectively and consistently than to react in every instance. It is better to ignore than to respond inconsistently. At first, you will need to get used to this objective, non-emotional method and learn that fewer responses are judicious. The frequently repeated misbehaviors require action before the infrequent ones. Both parents should agree on the top-five list of misbehaviors and first focus on them. When the first five come under control, you may shift the focus.

Be Brief

Always be brief and leave no room for argument. "You've done this, it is not allowed, and the consequence is..." **Never overexplain.** Children need to adjust their behaviors; they do not need to understand why! That will come naturally when they have sufficient reasoning powers and an experience base that makes the reason for your action clear.

Be Firm

Practice using a calm, non-emotional but firm voice. Sound as if there is no plea bargain, no wiggle room, and no chance of changing your mind. "No, do not do that. I expect you to color only in your coloring book, or on your plain paper, nowhere else. If you do, this (specific consequence) will happen."

Do Not Argue, Negotiate, or Overexplain

Arguing, negotiation, and overexplaining undermine and short-circuit the learning process. It delays and weakens the necessary urgent message that the behavior is not to be tolerated. It gives your child a chance to change the outcome and weakens the lesson that s/he has made a poor choice. It sends the message to the child that if s/he continues to talk, the rule will be changed and s/he will *not* suffer the consequences. Arguing, negotiating, and explaining are *NOT* a consequence. Children usually learn if a consequence follows their choice.

Limit Warnings

If the activity is dangerous (a Law): "No, that is dangerous. Stop," is sufficient. If the child continues the activity, a consequence swiftly follows. If it has to do with a Rule (personal rights and property rights): "You are about to break a rule; respect others' rights/property," is also sufficient. In addressing the SOP's (manners) "stay out of that; please do this or that," is the example. A second reminder is okay for children under four years old.

After age four to five years. once is enough! Multiple warnings are ineffective and send the message that you don't really mean what you say.

Be Practical

Children learn best when the consequence quickly follows their misbehavior. At home, it is easier to follow through than it is in the mall, restaurant, church, or grocery store.

Creativity and flexibility are needed. Consequences vary with the age: two-, four-, seven-, and twelve-year-olds require different approaches. Outside the home, misdeeds need to be handled at the time, not later when children will have forgotten the circumstances and the consequences will be less meaningful. You may have to remove them from the store, mall, or restaurant to calm them down and to receive their consequence.

Be Composed and Calm

Remove the emotion from your response. When you are angry, you cannot think clearly, and it scares your children. They quit doing whatever it is because of your anger, not because of the lesson you want them to learn. Dispassionate correction and enforcement of consequences is your goal.

The outcome of discipline is to have the child learn. Regardless of the attitude your child displays after you impose the penalty, *do not waver.* Children often try to save face by saying hurtful things, i.e., "I don't love you, you don't love me, that's not fair," etc. Ignore their replies; your discipline will still be effective.

HELP SHEET #7

OVER-PARENTING QUIZ

Over-Parenting Quiz Questions About Your Child's Attitudes				
Part A	Answer Questions with Yes Sometimes No **Does Your Child:**	Yes	Sometimes	No
1	Attempt to sway your response with "that's not fair?"			
2	Refuse to do difficult tasks?			
3	Delay, pout or refuse to do chores?			
4	Expect a reward for anything you ask her/him to do?			
5	Blame others for his/her mistakes?			
6	Exhibit "end of the world" meltdowns when disappointed?			
7	Refuse to follow rules?			
8	Become upset when s/he doesn't win or isn't first?			
9	Expect you to make his/her life easier?			
10	Rarely say thank you for anything that you do for her/him?			
11	Demand treats when shopping?			
12	Give up easily?			
13	Hate to delay gratification?			
14	Act like you owe her/him something for anything s/he does to help?			
15	Act spoiled?			
Over-Parenting Quiz Are you A Helicopter or Lawnmower Parent?				
Part B	Answer Questions with Yes Sometimes No **DO YOU:**	Yes.	Sometimes	No
1	Fix your child's difficulties?			
2	Hesitate before you ask your child to do something because s/he will complain?			
3	Constantly remind your child to do chores but there is no consequence?			

4	Make excuses for your child's failures and shortcomings?			
5	Say your child is the most important thing in your life?			
6	Frequently argue with your child?			
7	Brag to your friends about your child's accomplishments?			
8	Arrange more than one afterschool activity per week?			
9	Allow your child to play alone (under three years) in the house (over three) outside the house?			
10	Help your child settle disagreements with her/his friends?			
11	Check your child's homework?			
	Are you a Helicopter or Lawnmower Parent?			
	Question	Yes.	Sometimes	No
12	Have a functioning nanny cam?			
13	Frequently remind your child of the safety rules?			
14	Check and arrange your child's backpack?			
15	Always take your child's side when criticized by others?			
16	Say "My child would never do that?"			
17	Frequently let your child win playing games?			
18	Frequently step in to prevent your child from making a mistake?			
19	Frequently worry about your child's happiness?			
20	Give your child a gift because you feel guilty?			
21	Cringe when it is necessary to say "No" to your child?			
22	Frequently give in because your child wears you down?			
23	Rescue your child when he/she is in a jam?			
24	Frequently remind your child to do a job, finish a task, or complete a responsibility?			
25	Worry that your child won't like you?			
26	Buy too many presents for birthdays and Christmas to assure a better childhood than you had?			
27	Do things for your child s/he could do alone?			
28	Think when your child asks for something, "How soon can I get it?"			
29	Frequently buy your child a surprise treat to make them happy?			
30	Feel guilty if you contemplate *not doing* something for your children?			
31	Feel guilty when you ask your child to do you a favor?			
32	Find yourself doing things for your child because your friends do the same for their child?			

33	Give your child more things they want than he/she earns?			
34	Regularly attempt to neutralize your child's failures?			
35	Tell your children how to solve a problem more often than you ask them how they are going to solve it?			
	Total			

Not-so-easy children are, by their temperament and executive function deficits, less resilient and at risk for anxiety, depression, social problems and/or learning issues. Adding over-parenting in the form of helicoptering and lawn mowing increases the likelihood of these mental health issues becoming significant problems and struggles in the child's teen years. Corrective measures are needed.

Questionnaire scoring

Scoring Yes = 2 points Sometimes = 1 point No = 0 points

Child questionnaire

Total points

- **5 – 10** Your child is set up and ready for entitlement
- **10 - 20** Your child is showing struggles and probable anxiety
- **>20** Your child is struggling with the full effects of poor coping skills

Parent questionnaire

Total points

- **10 - 20** On-call Hovering parent
- **20 - 40** Full time Rescuing Helicopter parent
- **>40** Relentless Medivac Helicopter parent

HELP SHEET #8

Ten Parenting Pearls

Pearls are formed by irritants within a mollusk's shell. These pearls are formed by my years of helping parents deal with the irritants of raising their children. They are meant to help you fulfill your goal as a parent in helping your child to become a happy and successful adult.

1. Forget about *making* your child happy!

It is impossible to *make* someone else truly happy. Happiness comes with a good ice cream cone, but that feeling is fleeting. Your child's long-term happiness isn't your responsibility. Happiness is a journey and a process of learning who you are and developing the resilience to deal with and appreciate all that comes your way. Life's challenges come at us like a series of waves and keep coming. They buffet, overwhelm and can knock us off our feet. Some parents begin their parenting career trying to stop the waves, only to realize that is impossible. As the meditation teacher and author Jon Kabat Zinn said, "You can't stop the waves, but you can learn to surf."

2. Praise effort, not success.

All children need and benefit from praise. They love encouragement. They drink it up and grow from it. Give your child lots of encouragement and praise. "***You** must be proud of yourself! You really worked hard.*" This praise should be for them. Saying,

"I'm proud of you" only places you in the accomplishment and they are then sharing their accomplishment with you. Don't take credit unless you also want to take the blame when things don't go well. You don't want your children doing well only to please you. Do not allow their achievements to determine their or your self-worth.

3. Allow your child to take all the responsibility.

Let your children devise their own method for remembering what needs to be done, or let them ask you for help rather than telling them what they need to do. Don't tie your five-year-old's shoes when she can tie her own or dress her when she can dress herself. Avoid hovering and holding her back from normal "risks" a child would take at her age level. It's also not a good idea to talk to her teachers incessantly. If she hesitates to make her own decisions, try not to jump in and do it for her; let her reason it out on her own if she can. Allow her to feel discomfort or pain: it's part of growing up. Don't prevent her from struggling or rescue her from life's hardships. Naturally, parents want to keep their kids safe, but eliminating all risk robs kids of learning resiliency. Precious teachers are those most difficult problems children struggle to solve. These often become some of the most prized lessons we ever learn.

4. Don't make your child the center of your world.

If you are constantly on-call, your child is not managing his own life—you are. What happens when you are not there? Do not focus on your child and imagine all the worst outcomes. Quit worrying about his self-esteem. Relax and let him figure it out. I have confidence he will, and he will feel great about doing it himself. Let go of constant worry and realize you can't control everything your kids do. You cannot remove all the risks. You can only respond to what happens next. Letting go of expectations and worries will help you become a calmer, more peaceful parent. Your child will grow unencumbered without your constant presence.

5. Eat as many meals together as possible.

The American family needs a center to grow, interact as a group, and be together to learn from one another. Mealtime is that time. Taking turns around the table for all family members to talk is important for connection and social growth. Many times, children will speak out about what happened during the day in this context, but say, "Oh nothing," when you ask, "What happened at school today." The social function of meals is as important as the nutritional one.

6. Decrease all screen time for the *entire* family.

People today are losing human contact and, with it, their empathy. Recent research studies have proven empathy for others goes down when screen time goes up. Enforce "no screens," at mealtime and during all shared time. Be in the moment when you are with your kids. That office email or text can wait until they are in bed. When was the last time you just sat and listened to your child? Kids say that their number-one wish is to spend more time with their parents and that they really listen.

7. Have Fun. Act silly.

Let yourself be playful, have fun, be unconventional, be totally wacko occasionally. Introduce novelty into the day; everyone loves novelty. Children respond to it with enthusiasm. Your child is full of life and loves to play. Play, recent research has shown, is a great teacher. Too much of their lives involves structure, schedules, lists, and rules: just like yours, demands and more demands. Show them that having fun has an important place in life. Healthy families also need parents to set aside time for their mutual nurturing. Marriages are stressed today with a multitude of demands, but when no time is planned together, moms and dads drift apart. Single parents also need time with friends for fun and support. Lose the guilt about nurturing yourself.

8. Appreciate your children for their uniqueness.

It sounds trite, but parents too commonly are trying to give every advantage, maximize their children's exposure to all the best things, and strive to make their children the "best they can be." Appreciating kindness, generosity, creativity, and honesty gets lost. Communication, artistic talent, listening, analytical thinking, interpersonal communication, planning/organizing skill, reasoning, and teamwork go unappreciated. However, these very traits will most likely play a role in what each child will become and how successful she will be. Providing all the *"right"* opportunities is not necessarily the best course for a child. Developing, expanding, and enhancing who they are provides the best outcome.

9. Treat all your child's failures as successes.

Many parents today spend an enormous amount of effort attempting to keep their children from screwing up. Even if you are successful that is a recipe for long term parenting failure! Children only learn by failing, suffering a consequence and learning how to solve that problem when it recurs. Building resilience is an exercise in learning how to solve problems. Each time your children fail they learn. Stay calm when they fail, don't give it undue importance. Your responsibility is only to say, "Well, that didn't turn out so well, what are you going to do next time?" If perfectionism is a trait you are working on read, *The Gift of Failure* by Jessica Lahey.

10. Become a "Good enough parent."

This concept comes first from D.W. Winnicott, FRCP, an early twentieth century English pediatrician, and later by Bruno Bettelheim in his book, *A Good Enough Parent.* The concept is that good enough parents do not attempt to be perfect parents, nor do they expect perfection from their kids. Having a perfectionistic expectation leads to blaming. Blaming themselves, the child, the other parent, the teacher, or circumstances. Blame doesn't help the child learn to solve problems. Blame is destructive and prevents addressing the real issues. Good enough parents focus on the child's learning experiences and builds a foundation of problem solving. Good enough parents provide help for their children to meet their needs and are good reality sounding boards. They do not become ever-present fixers, rescuers, or interferers of learning. Good enough parents believe good enough is great.

Enjoy your child now—yesterday is gone and tomorrow is not here!

TEAR AND SHARE SHEETS

1. NSEC Rating Scale
2. Over-Parenting Quiz
3. Behavioral Cascade
4. Laws, Rules, and SOP's
5. Behaviors and Remedies

Not-so-easy child (NSEC) Rating Scale

NSEC rating scale score for your child is measured by the number of challenges she/he give you in a given time period. A challenge is defined as anything that causes you frustration, drives you a little nutty or creates a fit throwing melt down by your child or you. This can be a refusal to obey, a tantrum, a crying fit, when she/he is frustrated. A challenge can be resistance to a request, defiance, refusal to try anything new, or anything that causes you to be interrupted in your flow of the day. If your child gives you a challenge two times every month she/he would fit in the second box, occasionally challenging, and you select the number below like 3 or 4. If your child causes you to be frustrated every day, then you would circle 9 or 10 which equals a very, very Not-so-easy child.

VERY EASY		EASY		NOT SO EASY		VERY NOT SO EASY		VERY VERY NOT SO EASY	
Never Challenging		Occasionally Challenging		Regularly Challenging		Frequently Challenging		Always Challenging	
Challenges over time									
0-1/month		1-3/month		Weekly		1-3/week		Daily	
Select the Number below that matches This Child's Rating of Challenges over time.									
1	2	3	4	5	6	7	8	9	10

Now you know that you have a NSEC and with a 5 or a 9 score you could use some help. There are many other labels associated with these children: strong-willed, defiant, difficult, behaviorally challenged, high maintenance, demanding, high spirited, head strong, troubled, temperamental and spoiled. I believe that "Not-so-easy child" is a kinder phrase to use to refer to these interesting kids. What makes them NSE? We will discuss this in detail using the new neuroscience that helps explain how your children are wired and what makes them tick and causes their alarms to go off.

OVER-PARENTING QUIZ

Over-Parenting Quiz Questions About Your Child's Attitudes				
Part A	Answer Questions with Yes Sometimes No **Does Your Child:**	Yes	Sometimes	No
1	Attempt to sway your response with "that's not fair?"			
2	Refuse to do difficult tasks?			
3	Delay, pout or refuse to do chores?			
4	Expect a reward for anything you ask her/him to do?			
5	Blame others for his/her mistakes?			
6	Exhibit "end of the world" meltdowns when disappointed?			
7	Refuse to follow rules?			
8	Become upset when s/he doesn't win or isn't first?			
9	Expect you to make his/her life easier?			
10	Rarely say thank you for anything that you do for her/him?			
11	Demand treats when shopping?			
12	Give up easily?			
13	Hate to delay gratification?			
14	Act like you owe her/him something for anything s/he does to help?			
15	Act spoiled?			

Over-Parenting Quiz Are you A Helicopter or Lawnmower Parent?				
Part B	Answer Questions with Yes Sometimes No **DO YOU:**	Yes.	Sometimes	No
1	Fix your child's difficulties?			
2	Hesitate before you ask your child to do something because s/he will complain?			
3	Constantly remind your child to do chores but there is no consequence?			

4	Make excuses for your child's failures and shortcomings?			
5	Say your child is the most important thing in your life?			
6	Frequently argue with your child?			
7	Brag to your friends about your child's accomplishments?			
8	Arrange more than one afterschool activity per week?			
9	Allow your under three y/o child to play alone without constant supervision inside the house and over 3y/o outside the house in a safe yard?			
10	Help your child settle disagreements with her/his friends?			
11	Check your child's homework?			
	Are you a Helicopter or Lawnmower Parent?			
	Question	Yes.	Sometimes	No
12	Have a functioning nanny cam?			
13	Frequently remind your child of the safety rules?			
14	Check and arrange your child's backpack?			
15	Always take your child's side when criticized by others?			
16	Say "My child would never do that?"			
17	Frequently let your child win playing games?			
18	Frequently step in to prevent your child from making a mistake?			
19	Frequently worry about your child's happiness?			
20	Give your child a gift because you feel guilty?			
21	Cringe when it is necessary to say "No" to your child?			
22	Frequently give in because your child wears you down?			
23	Rescue your child when he/she is in a jam?			
24	Frequently remind your child to do a job, finish a task, or complete a responsibility?			
25	Worry that your child won't like you?			
26	Buy too many presents for birthdays and Christmas to assure a better childhood than you had?			
27	Do things for your child s/he could do alone?			

28	Think when your child asks for something, "How soon can I get it?"			
29	Frequently buy your child a surprise treat to make them happy?			
30	Feel guilty if you contemplate *not doing* something for your children?			
31	Feel guilty when you ask your child to do you a favor?			
32	Find yourself doing things for your child because your friends do the same for their child?			
33	Give your child more things they want than he/she earns?			
34	Regularly attempt to neutralize your child's failures?			
35	Tell your children how to solve a problem more often than you ask them how they are going to solve it?			
	Total			

Not-so-easy children are, by their temperament and executive function deficits, less resilient and at risk for anxiety, depression, social problems and/or learning issues. Adding over-parenting in the form of helicoptering and lawn mowing increases the likelihood of these mental health issues becoming significant problems and struggles in the child's teen years. Corrective measures are needed.

Questionnaire scoring

Scoring Yes = 2 points Sometimes = 1 point No = 0 points

Child questionnaire

Total points

5 – 10 Your child is set up and ready for entitlement

10 - 20 Your child is showing struggles and probable anxiety

>20 Your child is struggling with the full effects of poor coping skills

Parent questionnaire

Total points

10 - 20	On-call Hovering parent
20 - 40	Full time Rescuing Helicopter parent
>40	Relentless Medivac Helicopter parent

The three phases of this failed response to completing and solving a problem are as follows. First, lock up; second, meltdown; and third, lash out.

Phase I Lock Up

When it becomes evident to the child that his one answer to the problem is not going to work and his only other reaction is to shut down. The first thing that occurs when children are overwhelmed is that they lock up. During the lock-up phase, their brain is engaged and still working, so they can solve the problem with help. We all know a child's lock-up face: pouting lips, frowning forehead, crossed arms, and generally unhappy demeanor. The less emotional we are as parents, the better we can help the child solve the problem and not fulfill the rest of the cascade. But, often at this phase, the child is pushed to rapidly solve the problem by either himself, his parents, his teacher, or a sibling or friend.

During this phase their brain is still open, aware and capable of solving a problem with a little help. This is the ONLY time you can intervene with success.

Phase II Meltdown

This is the natural next phase if Phase I is not resolved, or a parent, sib, or teacher continues to push the child to solve the problem. When children are pushed, they move to the next phase of this cascade, which is meltdown. When they are in the meltdown phase, their brain disengages and they cannot solve the problem. This looks like anything from crying to a full-fledged, foot-stomping, throwing-themselves-on-the-floor fit. When we become angry and upset, we lose IQ points; the experts say as many as fifty points. Most of us would have a hard time solving any problem down fifty IQ points. This is the point where things can really escalate and get ugly, if the parent attempts to stop the meltdown. However, when you push a locked-up child to "do it now," or to "hurry up," you just pushed him into a meltdown (what I call the mudhole). Picture yourself crawling down into a mudhole. When you try to stop a meltdown, you are figuratively getting into the mudhole with your child. Nothing good or clean comes out of the mudhole. If the child has gotten to the meltdown phase, stay away from the machinery, it is too late to help. Allow the meltdown to run its course. After calm has been established say, "Wow, you didn't solve that problem, let's start over.

Phase III Lashing Out

This occurs when there is continued interaction with the child and she is not left to calm down. The child will lash out with aggressive verbal or physical behavior. Usually what happens next is lashing out. The child spits, calls you names, claws, kicks, bites, throws things, says he doesn't love you, and generally goes totally berserk. This is most commonly accompanied by a yelling and screaming parent. The parent is lashing out, too. Everyone suffers. Overall, a nasty, scary sight. Occasionally, more violence follows, and the child is spanked or punished. Whew, that requires a lot of energy and leaves everybody drained. Guilt follows.

All because your child was struggling with solving a problem, and usually someone tried to intervene. The child was being driven by his temperament overwhelming him, not because the child intentionally misbehaved. No one would get mad and react angrily to a child who cannot hear who throws a fit because she cannot understand a problem. So why do we commonly react in this frustrated, angry way with our own children? Remember, a meltdown means the brain is disengaged and cannot solve the problem at hand. The best advice is to allow the meltdown to run its course without any intervention or discussion. After the child has calmed down, calmly revisit by helping the child to solve the problem.

After you comprehend the behavior drivers and the brain wiring of your child, it will be much easier to facilitate a problem-solving, non-fit-throwing experience. The resilient child rarely has a meltdown and infrequently locks up. The less resilient the child, the more often he or she locks up, and experiences a meltdown, or lashes out. Once parents can revise the myth that the child's behavior is intentional, their frustration and anger is replaced with empathy, and guilt vanishes.

We know that there are learning drivers, as well as behavioral ones. When children do not remember what you told them to do the day before, they are not intentionally ignoring you, but rather are having trouble hearing information and getting it stored in their memory for recall later. It is much harder in the learning process to hear information and store it than it is to see information and store it. That is why most schools have smart boards and there is much more visual learning than ever before. If you have a child who is a visual learner and his teacher gives directions verbally, the child will struggle in that classroom. The child is not being lazy; the child is not cognitively challenged, but rather he is struggling with some of his executive functions.

The more we understand and identify children's temperament traits and executive functions, the better equipped we are to help a child who struggles with his behavior and learning.

FAMILY STRUCTURE BOUNDARIES

LAWS: Safety issues that could hurt you or someone else.

(Capital Crimes, the most serious offense)

CONSEQUENCE: The major lesson for putting oneself or another person in harm's way is to learn why it is dangerous! The consequence is to imprint the lesson, not to punish. Do not get mad no matter how scared the act made you; that could shift the child's focus to pleasing the parent rather than learning the danger lesson. The consequence for breaking the Law is "imprisonment" called the *Think Tank*. One minute per year of age until 5, then 5–10 minutes for all older children. The think tank should be located somewhere there is nothing to do but think about the law broken. The best chair in the living room is OK and a contrast to the tub in tub time. This is a little different from time out, in that after the timer goes off you have a discussion with your child about why what he did was dangerous. (In time out no discussion; after time out, the time isolated requires no explanation.)

Always be consistent
Immediate action, without emotion

Consequence for breaking the same law within an hour or refusing to go to the think tank is loss of next major opportunity, outing, sports event, sleep over, special event with friend.

Protect yourself and others from harm by:

- Not running in house.
- Not climbing or jumping on furniture, in bathtub, on bed.
- Not hitting, kicking, pinching, biting, pushing people or pets.
- Not playing near or in street.
- Not crossing street without adult.
- Not going to friend's house or anywhere without permission.
- Not throwing things in house, including food.
- Not throwing things at people or animals.
- Staying with Mom and Dad during excursions.
- Not opening doors for anyone other than family or friends approved by parents.
- Not talking to strangers without parent's permission.
- Not playing with knives.
- Always wear seatbelts in *ALL* cars.
- Not eating and playing at the same time.
- Anything else deemed **unsafe** by parents at the time it occurs.

- Do not take any medicines, drugs, beer, wine, or alcohol or huff aerosols.
- Older children & adolescents need age appropriate refinements of these laws.

RULES: Personal Rights & Property Rights (Felonies)

Personal Rights/Freedoms:

- Personal space rights: (Children with high sensory thresholds have significant issues with others space and require you to be more vigilant)
- Everyone has an 18" space around him or her that is private and should not be invaded without permission. (Except for hugs and kisses, when accepted willingly.)
- *Everyone has the right to have peace in his or her space with minimal noise and confusion.*
- Everyone has space that is private, such as rooms, drawers, closets, etc., and should not be entered without permission. (Parents can override this for any safety reason.)

Personal time rights:

- Everyone has the right to be alone and have time in her/his space with minimal noise and confusion.

Play rights:

- All children have the right to play in any means that is safe, considerate of others' rights, and with permission of parents.

Activity rights:

- Children have the right to participate in any organized activities (sports, dance, music, Scouts, lessons, sleepovers, campouts, & others) with parent's approval and support.

Property Rights:

Children have the right to own and care for property, including toys, games, books, clothes, electronics, and equipment.

CONSEQUENCE: Loss of a previously awarded privilege (TV, computer, electronic game, or telephone time) or removal of property (favorite toy, game, book).

Individualized for each child by making a list of the top 3 favorite things to do (personal rights) and 3 top favorite possessions (property rights). These are then removed in order of importance or reverse order in the nonadaptive child.

Consequence for breaking the same law within an hour or refusing to go to the think tank is loss of next major opportunity, outing, sports event, sleep over, special event with friend.

Personal rights:

- Respect = Do not physically invade others' personal or private space.
- Respect = Do not invade others' personal space with noise and confusion.
- Respect = Do not interrupt others' private time.
- Respect = Do not disrupt others' play.

- Respect = Meeting responsibilities to others involved in activities (practicing, being on time, participating to fullest).

Property rights:
Failure to care for property automatically qualifies for removal of that property by the parents for a set period of time or forever depending on past care of belongings.

- Respect = Not taking things that are not yours. (No stealing.)
- Respect = Not destroying or messing up others' property. (No vandalism.)
- Respect = Not taking things away from people.
- Respect = Not bothering or playing with others' possessions without permission.
- Respect = Not bothering or playing with parent controlled electronic equipment (TV, VCR, CD player, computers, printers, etc.)

SOPs: Personal Responsibilities, manners & social conventions (misdemeanors)

CONSEQUENCE: Removal of a pleasure or treat, additional one-time chore, impose a fine.

Personal responsibilities:

- Dress self.
- Put up your clothes in proper place.
- Put dirty clothes and linens in laundry bin.

- Put away toys before changing activities and at the end of every day.
- Wipe, flush toilet, & close lid.
- Wash hands before and after eating.
- Sleep or play quietly in room during rest/quiet time.
- Wash face in the morning, in the evening, and after eating.
- Go to bed on time.
- Brush teeth and floss twice a day.
- Come when called.
- Make your bed every morning as soon as you get up.

Manners:

- Say please and thank you.
- Shake hands when meeting people.
- Look people in the eyes when you are talking to them.
- Don't pick your nose in public.
- Use a napkin at the table.
- Use a Kleenex to wipe your nose.
- Don't play with food.
- Do not yell at people.
- Treat all others as you want to be treated.
- All other things parents want to add.

Chores: Defined as any job that benefits the family. *Returning to a family-centered instead of a child-centered family requires that all members contribute to the well-being of the family. That means sharing the tasks of managing a home. Everyone helps. Explain to your children that being a member of the family has responsibilities and privileges. The chore always precedes the privilege. "Fist the chore, then the freedom/privilege! Regular* *chores increase competence and the feeling of being needed, the last two requirements for self-esteem.*

Guidelines for Chores:

1. Start chores at an early age. Eighteen months to two years is perfect.
2. Show your children how to do the chore in detail, have them repeat it a few times to be assured they understand. Be specific. (Clean your room is vague, be specific.) Clean your room means to pick up all toys, clothes, books, shoes and put in the proper place.
3. Write and post the list in a place for family communication. (Refrigerator, bulletin board, shared computer scheduler, etc.)
4. Introduce one chore at a time with the when/then rule. (When the chores are done, then you can have free time.) Responsibilities always come before rights.
5. The first part of the chore is the chore, and the second part of all chores is a definitive time for completion. (Take out the trash is half a chore; take out the trash by 7:00PM is a full chore.) At 7:01 if the trash is still in the basket the child did not do that chore and the consequence is given. No excuses or discussions.
6. Increase the number and complexity of chores as the child grows and develops. See chart below. (I often hear how smart your children are by learning to operate complex electronics to using complex thinking; don't excuse that child from learning how to turn on a dishwasher!)

7. Monitor inconspicuously at first. *Never redo your child's task.* (The results will improve with practice; if they don't, have another learning session.)
8. Do not remind or nag.
9. Do not do the chore for them when they forget or refuse.
10. Provide preset consequences for failure to do the chore.
11. Consequences should be logical extensions of the chore. For example, if the child doesn't
    a. Put away her/his bike, the bike is impounded for a day.
    b. Remind the children that the family counts on them to do this chore for the family.
    c. Rights have responsibilities, and they must balance.
    d. When a responsibility (chore) is not completed, they forfeit a right. Another consequence for failure to do a chore can be another chore. (These chores may come from a list that is a non-regular extra chore, as raking leaves, cleaning the garage, etc., that normally is bid on and payment is received, except when a consequence no payment is made. It is a paid chore done for free!)

Age appropriate chores:

- Under 3: start with the above listed personal responsibilities.

- Ages 3 to 5 years old: can set and clear table, clean spills, empty wastebaskets, bring in mail, clear table, pull weeds, hand vacuum to pick up solid spills, unload utensils from dishwasher, get their own drinks and fix a bowl of cereal.

- Ages 6-7: Above plus sort laundry, sweep floors, set table, make snacks of cold foods, PB &J sandwiches, rake leaves, answer telephone and take messages.

- Ages 8-9: Above plus load dishwasher, put away groceries, vacuum and dust, fold and put away laundry, peel vegetables, cook simple food (toast, microwave), mop floor, mow yard with supervision.

- Ages 10-12: Above plus clean bathrooms, wash windows, wash car, iron their clothes, do family laundry, cook simple meals with supervision, bake dcookies, younger sib care, have neighborhood jobs (mow yards, pet care, etc.).

- Over 12 years: Above plus most any task an adult can do. At sixteen and after six months' driving experience, adolescents can run errands, such as picking up laundry/ dry cleaning, grocery shopping, etc., and be completely responsible for family meals once or twice a week.

START SMALL, BUT START! YOU AND YOUR CHILDREN MAY BE PLEASANTLY SURPRISED AT YOUR ABILITY TO WORK AND PLAY TOGETHER AS A FAMILY.

BEHAVIORS AND REMEDIES

Over the years parents have regularly asked for examples of specific behavior to be matched with specific consequences. Here are the examples using the Modified Eyberg Behavior Inventory

Adapted from the Modified Eyberg Child Behavior Inventory*

1. Takes too long to dress in the morning ∞ Take the child to the required location (school) in the current state of dress with clothes and shoes in a bag.
2. Takes too long to eat a meal ∞ Set a timer of maximal time for the meal = how long parents stay at the table
3. Has poor manners ∞ Teach them manners and expect results or give consequences
4. Refuses to eat many foods ∞ Introduce new foods slowly, (see withdrawing behavior under Temperament)
5. Refuses to do chores when asked ∞ Administer consequence
6. Slow getting ready for bed ∞ Have a routine that is time sensitive allowing 30 minutes of private time prior to lights out
7. Refuses to go to bed on time ∞ Administer consequence if you are certain it isn't anxiety that is the root of failure to sleep, (see body clock irregularity)
8. Does not obey rules ∞ Administer preset consequences

9.Refuses to obey even when threatened ∞ Don't threaten; give consequences instead

10. Acts defiant when told to do something ∞ See nonadaptable temperament

11. Argues with parents and teachers about rules ∞ Do not argue. First ignore, and if it persists administer consequence.

12. Gets angry when child doesn't get his/her way ∞ The child is not solving the problem (see Transition time help sheet.)

13. Has temper tantrums ∞ Do not engage, after cool down either problem solve or ignore

14. Sasses adults ∞ Ignore at first, and if persists administer consequence

15.Whines or Cries easily ∞ Ignore, (see negative mood.)

16.Yells or Screams at others ∞ Don't tolerate, administer consequence, then problem solve

17. Hits parents ∞ Lashing out (see Behavioral Cascade) When calm, problem solve

18. Destroys or is careless with toys ∞ Do not replace and remove a different one for a day as the consequence

19.Steals ∞ Administer appropriate consequence

20.Lies ∞ First, is it defensive lying "chocolate on the mouth syndrome" which you caused? Back up and start over. If not defensive, administer appropriate consequence. Don't over react

21. Teases or picks on other children ∞ Don't tolerate, administer consequences, then problem solve

22. Has shouting matches with sibs or friends ∞ Don't tolerate, administer consequences, then problem solve

23. Physically fights with sibs or friends ∞ Don't tolerate, administer consequences, then problem solve

24. Constantly seeks attention ∞ Problem solve how to play alone
25. Interrupts often ∞ See impulse control options
26. Is easily distracted ∞ See impulse control options
27. Has a short attention span ∞ See impulse control, persistent, distraction options
28. Fails to finish jobs or homework ∞ See impulse control, persistent, distraction options
29.Cannot seem to concentrate on one thing ∞ See impulse control, persistent, distraction options
30. Is overactive or restless ∞ Give plenty of active time, use active consequences before reboot time
31. Is shy ∞ See withdrawing temperament

Eyberg Behavioral Inventory https://clas.uiowa.edu/sites/clas.uiowa.edu.nrcfcp/files/Eyberg%20Instrument.pdf

BIBLIOGRAPHY

Books Suggested to Help Parents of Not-so-easy Children

The Difficult Child by Stanley Turecki and L. Tonner. New York: Bantam Books, 1999 (Still one of the best books to understand temperament.)

The Explosive Child, third edition by Ross Greene, PhD, Harper Paperbacks, 2005

Child Behavioral Assessment and Management: Second Edition. William B. Carey, MD, & Sean C. McDevitt, PhD, Behavioral-Developmental Initiatives, 2016

Is That Me Yelling? A Parent's Guide to Getting Your Kids to Cooperate Without Losing Your Cool by Rona Renner. New Harbinger Publications, Inc., 2014

Is This a Phase? Child Development & Parent Strategies, Birth to 6 Years by Helen F. Neville Parenting Press, Jan 1, 2007

Understanding Your Child's Temperament. By William B. Carey, M.D., with Martha M. Jablow. New York. Macmillan: Simon & Schuster, 2005

The Highly Sensitive Child: Helping Our Children Thrive When the World Overwhelms them. By Elaine N. Aron, Broadway Books, 2002

Temperament tools: Working with Your Child's Inborn Trait by Helen Neville and Diane Clark Johnson. Parenting Press, Inc., 1997

The Challenging Child by Standley Greenspan, MD, Da Capo Press, 1995

Raising Your Spirited Child by Mary Sheedy Kurchinka Harper Perennial Press, 1991

Hamlet's Blackberry by William Powers Harper Perennial; Reprint edition (August 9, 2011)

The narcissism epidemic living in the age of entitlement by Jean M Twenge PhD and W Keith Campbell PhD Atria Books; unknown edition (April 13, 2010)

Generation Me - Revised and updated: Why Today's Young Americans Are More Confident, Assertive, Entitled--and More Miserable than Ever Before by Jean Twenge, PhD Atria Books; revised, updated ed. edition (September 2014)

IGEN: why today's super-connected kids are growing up less rebellious, more tolerant, less happy--and completely unprepared for adulthood--and what that means for the rest of us by Jean Twenge, PhD Atria Books; revised, updated ed. edition (September 2018)

The Learning Brain Memory and Brain Development in Children by Torkel Klingberg Oxford University Press; 1 Edition (November 2, 2012)

How to raise an adult Break Free all the over parenting trap and prepare your kid for success by Julie Lynncott Hakim St. Martin's Griffin; Reprint edition (August 2, 2016)

Smart parenting for smart kids by Eileen Kennedy Moore & Mark S Lowenthal Ossey-Bass; 1 edition (March 1, 2011)

Play: How it Shapes the Brain, Opens the Imagination and Invigorates the Soul by Stuart Brown, MD with Christopher Vaughn Avery (1822)

Grit The power of passion and perseverance by Angela Duckworth Scribner; Reprint edition (August 21, 2018)

The Overflowing Brain by Torkel Klingberg Oxford University Press; 1 edition (November 7, 2008)

What if everybody understood child development? By Rea Pica Orwin; 1 edition (May 6, 2015)

The Gift of Failure: How the Best Parents Learn to Let Go so Their Children Can Succeed by Jessica Lahey Harper; Reprint edition (August 11, 2015)

The Price of Privilege by Madaline Levine, PhD

Choking on the Silver Spoon by Gary W. Bufford, PhD

Nurture Shock by Po Bronson Ashley Merryman, "How Not to Talk to Kids" and "The Inverse Power of Praise"

Tulsa World: "Helicopter Parenting" Posted Monday, March 24, 2014 12:00 am | Updated: Mon Mar 24, 2014

Kahlil Gibran *Your Children Are Not Your Children*

There is life after college by Jeffrey J Selingo William Morrow Paperbacks; Reprint edition (April 4, 2017)

Where you go is not who you'll be and anecdote to college admissions mania by Frank Bruni Grand Central Publishing; Updated, Expanded edition (March 8, 2016)

http://www.katsandogz.com/onchildren.html

Books for the parent of an older children/teens

The Boogeyman Exists; And He's in Your Child's Back Pocket: Internet Safety Tips For Keeping Your Children Safe Online, Smartphone Safety, Social Media Safety, and Gaming Safety. Paperback, May 12, 2014 by Jesse Weinberger

Good Pictures Bad Pictures: Porn-Proofing Today's Young Kids. Paperback March 13, 2014 by Kristen A. Jenson M.A.

The Teenage Brain: A Neuroscientist's Survival Guide to Raising Adolescents and Young Adults Paperback, January 26, 2016 by Frances E. Jensen

Untangled: Guiding Teenage Girls Through the Seven Transitions into Adulthood. Hardcover, February 9, 2016 by Lisa Damour

Planet Middle School: Helping Your Child through the Peer Pressure, Awkward Moments & Emotional Drama. Hardcover, October 6, 2015 by Dr. Kevin Leman

GLOSSARY

A

Anxiety is the body's natural response to stress. It's a feeling of fear or apprehension about what's to come and is very common in NSEC, particularly the nonadaptable. These kids overcorrect by over planning and insisting on their plan which looks like they are trying to control everything.

ADD/ADHD is a medical diagnosis requiring the child to meet six of the nine symptoms of inattention and/or hyperactivity/impulsivity prior to age 12. Many children have less than the six required and do not meet the diagnosis of ADHD, but they need the same help. In the temperament/EF language ADD is working memory (cool EF) deficit without impulsivity and ADHD is with it. Any behavioral issues (hot EF) are NOT due to the diagnosis of ADHD but are separate issues requiring a different approach.

Adaptability is a temperament trait for the ability to shift, transition, and change according to the new needs of the situation. Nonadaptable children are less resilient and struggle with change.

Approach/withdrawal is a temperament trait with the ability to use new information. The withdrawing child is shy and resists new experiences, and the approaching child likes new experiences.

B

Behavior cascade is the less resilient phases a child exhibits when he is overwhelmed (stuck) by a problem he cannot solve. The three phases are: Lock up, Melt down and Lash out.

C

Consequences are natural outcomes or results of all actions. Some are good and some are not. They are life's teaching moments and are necessary for a child's healthy development. Failure to allow or impose consequences leads to dysfunctional development, later struggles, unhappiness and success in life.

Cool executive function is a classification of learning executive functions such as working memory.

Cognitive flexibility is the EF that incorporates the temperament traits of adaptability, approach/withdrawal, sensory threshold and mood to be able to shift direction, use new information and alter course as the situation changes.

E

Emotional control is the EF that incorporates the temperament traits of adaptability, approach/withdrawal, sensory threshold and mood and the EF of impulse control to achieve a balanced response to any situation.

Executive functions (EF) are the mental processing skills that enable us to inhibit impulses, shift directions when new information has changed our plan, control our emotions, retrieve information needed to solve problems, organize and manage time, focus attention, remember multiple steps, filter distractions, prioritize tasks, set and achieve goals and monitor our progress. All these skills are necessary to achieve self-regulation and obtain success. The three hot EF (behavioral drivers) are: Inhibitory Control, Cognitive Flexibility, Emotional Control. The five cool EF are: Initiation, Working Memory, Plan/Organize, Organize Materials, Monitoring.

Executive dysfunction is the new medical term for executive function deficits that lead to behavioral and or learning problems.

F

Fit is a concept of parent/child interaction compatibility. Temperament traits of parent and child can mesh or clash. If they mesh it is a good fit; if it clashes it is a poor fit and conflict occurs.

H

Helicoptering is a dysfunctional style of parenting by constant hovering and swooping in to fix any difficulties or possible failures.

Hyperactivity is a state of high activity of energy, constant movement and talking.

High sensory threshold is the lack or poor appreciation of sensory signals, high pain threshold, less empathy for others and often includes social communication issues.

Hot executive function is the classification of behavioral executive functions comprised of inhibitory control, cognitive flexibility, and emotional control.

I

I expect is the phrase to use first and every time you want your child to do something and always with a time to complete, such as: "I expect you to put on your shoes in five minutes," and a timer is set.

Impulse control is a more common term for the executive function Inhibition Control.

Inhibition control is the denotation of the executive function, meaning the same as impulse control and is the EF that allows a child to inhibit or ignore distractions, to focus and to stay on task.

Initiation is the cool EF that marks the ability to start a project. Those with weak initiation skills are said to procrastinate. Procrastination is not a moral habit but in fact is a lack of EF skill and an executive dysfunction.

J

Just right parenting is the goal of being a parent who is easily accessible without being constantly present. The ability to help a child learn and build skill sets without doing it for them or making it easier by removing all obstacles. It is a teaching parent who responds rather that reacts and responds with as little emotion to misbehavior as possible.

L

Lash out is the last phase of the behavioral cascade (Mudhole experience) that results from trying to stop a meltdown. The child becomes uncontrollable and may call you names, hit, bite, kick and lash out and say he doesn't love you anymore. His brain ceases to function enough to solve a problem and stops working properly.

Lawnmower parent is a dysfunctional style of parenting by constantly removing any obstacle in the child's path that may pose difficulties or possible failures for the child.

Laws rules and SOP's is my structure to family life and is like capital crimes, felonies and misdemeanors. These expectations are written, posted with the consequences listed for failure to comply. This takes the guess work out of what you expect all the time and prevents on the spot coming up with a consequence.

Lock up is the first phase of the behavioral cascade when a child is signaling he is stumped, can't solve the problem and is about to explode. It is the only phase that you can be a part of by attempting to stop the cascade. (See Getting to Now What.)

Low sensory threshold is the temperament trait that registers sensory input. This end of the spectrum is the highly sensitive child who commonly is overwhelmed by loud, too tight, too smelly, too cold/hot, spicy or confusing. They are very empathetic and communicate well.

M

Meltdown is the second phase of the behavioral cascade when a child is being pushed to hurry, do it now, or fails to solve the problem. This phase is marked by a fit of varying degrees of yelling, throwing things and total brain shutdown. If allowed to run its course it will abate, but if there is an attempt to stop it usually goes to the last phase, lashing out.

Mood is the temperament trait that is either positive or negative, glass half full or half empty. Positive children sometimes fail to see the possible negative outcomes and the negative ones often fail to expect anything but negative outcome.

Monitoring is the last component of cool EF and denotes the ability to check one's work or her/his effect on others.

Mudhole is my expression for the end result of the behavioral cascade if not handled correctly and results in the parent and child losing it as they wallow in the mud for control. Both come out covered in anger, frustration, and for the parents, guilt, i.e. mud.

N

Nature vs Nurture are the influences of genetics and the environment.

Not-so-easy child is any child who is struggling to accomplish what is expected of him/her. The reasons vary with skills of temperament traits and EFs.

O

Organization materials is a cool EF trait that denotes the ability to organize his back pack, drawers, books, etc. If your child's back pack is a mess so are these skills.

Over-parenting is the style of being a parent that is ever present and includes both helicopters and lawnmowers (see above). This style arises in today's culture from intentions to be the best parent but has untoward consequences, causing teens and twenty somethings the inability to run their own lives and has resulted in one third of thirty-year-old's living at home!

P

Planning organization time management is one of the cool EF skills that enable complex tasks.

Punishment is what happens when parents get angry and wait too long to administer consequences. It is not a successful parenting action and rarely teaches, but often makes the child angry and resentful.

R

Reboot is the concept of starting over and the primary consequence for the NSEC.

Resilience is the characteristic of bouncing back or plasticity exhibited by children with balanced temperament traits and strong EFs. This is not only in large life experiences but in the day to day issues children face, such as when a toy is taken away by another child.

S

Self-regulation is the end product of strong EFs and balanced Temperament traits. It is the ability to calm yourself, handle frustration, adjust to a change and new information, and keep on task regardless of distractions to achieve your planned goals.

Sensory threshold is the temperament trait that reflects the strength of sensory input required for a child to pay attention. If only a small amount of cold or hot sensation is required for the child to notice, that child has a low threshold or is highly sensitive. The reverse is true if a large amount of input is required to notice a change, and that child would be classified as high threshold or less sensitive. The threshold measures the input to the five senses and is necessary to function.

T

Temperament traits are the inborn, genetically determined nine traits studied by Drs. Chess and Thomas. They are present at birth, measurable at 3 months and stable by age two years. They determine our first response or reaction to change, new experiences, sensory thresholds, our body clock regularity, activity level, persistence, distractibility and intensity and mood.

Timer is a mechanical or digital minute timer used to measure time to complete a task. The purpose is to set limits and remove the parent from the process of the child doing what was asked. It is set after the phrase, "I expect you to..."

Timeout is a frequently used default consequence for the under five-year-old.

W

Working memory is the important EF that is a child's brain's RAM and is responsible for temporarily retrieving and managing the information needed to solve complex cognitive tasks such as learning, and problem solving.

ABOUT THE AUTHOR

PHOTO BY NATALIE LEITER

Robert J. Hudson, MD, FAAP, Clinical Professor of Pediatrics with the University of Oklahoma School of Community Medicine, Tulsa. Dr. Hudson practiced general pediatrics for three decades and has devoted the past sixteen years as a behavioral pediatrician helping parents with children who exhibit behavioral or learning problems. He has completed early childhood research in public school PreK and kindergarten grades examining executive functions and how they affect behavior and learning.

Many of the parents who came for his behavioral counseling were at their wits end, full of guilt, feeling like parenting failures, but quickly learned how their child was wired, shifted their parenting approach by learning and applying new tools for managing their Not-so-easy child (NSEC). This book explores this same approach from toddler to teen's range of symptoms including; resistance, defiance, shyness, super sensitivity, anxiety, social issues, hyperactivity, attention problems, bullying, chronic unhappiness, impulsivity, compulsivity, distractibility, and chronic anger.

Dr. Hudson served as a consultant to public school districts and private school systems and was in demand for regional and national workshops to parents, teachers and professional groups.

Dr. Hudson has numerous honors and awards including:

- National Health Foundation Scholarship in Medicine
- Research Fellowship in Neurophysiology & Biochemistry
- Wyeth Pediatric Fellow in Pediatrics
- AMA Physicians in Radio and Television Award
- Undergraduate Rockefeller Scholarship
- American Association of Physician Executives

His website/blog, www.drbobsnsec.com continues helping parents with the complex world of raising children.

Made in the USA
Lexington, KY
20 April 2019